HOW TO CREATE A WEB3 STARTUP

A GUIDE FOR TOMORROW'S BREAKOUT COMPANIES

Tom Taulli

Foreword by Daniel Roberts

Apress®

How to Create a Web3 Startup: A Guide for Tomorrow's Breakout Companies

Tom Taulli
Monrovia, CA, USA

ISBN-13 (pbk): 978-1-4842-8682-1   ISBN-13 (electronic): 978-1-4842-8683-8
https://doi.org/10.1007/978-1-4842-8683-8

Managing Director, Apress Media LLC: Welmoed Spahr
Acquisitions Editor: Shiva Ramachandran
Development Editor: James Markham
Coordinating Editor: Jessica Vakili

Distributed to the book trade worldwide by Springer Science+Business Media New York, 1 New York Plaza, New York, NY 10004. Phone 1-800-SPRINGER, fax (201) 348-4505, e-mail orders-ny@springer-sbm.com, or visit www.springeronline.com. Apress Media, LLC is a California LLC and the sole member (owner) is Springer Science + Business Media Finance Inc (SSBM Finance Inc). SSBM Finance Inc is a **Delaware** corporation.

For information on translations, please e-mail booktranslations@springernature.com; for reprint, paperback, or audio rights, please e-mail bookpermissions@springernature.com.

Apress titles may be purchased in bulk for academic, corporate, or promotional use. eBook versions and licenses are also available for most titles. For more information, reference our Print and eBook Bulk Sales web page at http://www.apress.com/bulk-sales.

Printed on acid-free paper

Contents

About the Author

Tom Taulli has been developing software since the 1980s. In college, he started his first company, which focused on the development of e-learning systems. He created other companies as well, including Hypermart.net, which was sold to InfoSpace in 1996. Along the way, Tom has written columns for online publications such as BusinessWeek.com, TechWeb.com, and Bloomberg.com. He also writes posts on artificial intelligence for Forbes.com and is the adviser to various companies in the space. You can reach Tom on Twitter (@ttaulli) or through his website (www.tomtaulli.com).

About the Technical Reviewer

Stijn Van Hijfte has been working at Howest Applied University College since 2017, where he teaches applied computer science and is active as an expert at Sia Partners. He has a background in economics, IT, and data science and is often called in as a translator between business and IT departments. He started back in 2012 with some first investigations in the blockchain space and had his entire living room looking like a science experiment to connect to the Ethereum network in 2015. His continued interest in digital solutions has led to him studying many extra certifications and destroying equipment in the process.

Foreword

Web3 is weird.

Its biggest supporters spend their time advocating for their favorite crypto-currencies on Twitter and in Discord chat rooms, and proudly use cartoon NFT avatars (from Bored Apes to CryptoPunks to Cool Cats) as their profile pictures – before they flip them for profit and buy another one instead. Many of them proudly identify as members of token-specific camps, from "Bitcoin maximalists" to "Ethereans" to "LINK marines" to the "XRP army." They identify each other with in-crowd lingo like "gm," "WAGMI," "NGMI," "HODL," "down bad," and "rekt."

And yet, to dismiss Web3 as a passing fad (or, as crypto skeptics like to insist, a fraud or scam or Ponzi scheme) would be extremely short-sighted. It has already proven its staying power: Bitcoin has been trading for more than 13 years, and Ethereum for seven years, and neither blockchain has ever been hacked, nor has either coin ever gone to zero.

And after crypto had its biggest mainstream bull run yet in 2020 and 2021 during the pandemic, riding the retail investor revolution and Reddit-fueled meme stock wave, more big names are Web3 believers than ever before – both individuals and companies. Wall Street hedge fund titans changed their tune on crypto as an investment; publicly traded companies like Tesla and Square bought Bitcoin for their balance sheets; fintech giants like PayPal and Robinhood rolled out crypto buying features; consumer brands from Budweiser to Visa to Tiffany's to Gucci embraced NFTs.

All of this adds up to a very clear directive: Web3 is here to stay, and while it's still early days, the time to build is right now.

Coinbase was started in 2012 by a former Airbnb engineer and former Goldman Sachs trader; now it's publicly traded and a household name in the United States. Crypto exchange names and logos adorn the arenas of the LA Lakers and Miami Heat, and every MLB umpire's shirt. The CEO of DraftKings, the scrappy Boston startup that survived years of legal battles with state regulators to become a $10 billion sports betting behemoth, is a huge believer in crypto and told Decrypt this year: "Early in the internet days, there weren't a lot of mainstream ways to consume the internet… but everything eventually centered around the world wide web, all the underlying technology was built around that. And then all of a sudden things like video, and other things that are more mainstream and easier to consume for the average person, came about."

The economist and *New York Times* columnist Paul Krugman infamously wrote in 1998 that "the growth of the internet will slow drastically... By 2005 or so, it will become clear that the internet's impact on the economy has been no greater than the fax machine's." He was very, very wrong, and the quote resurfaces every few years to get roasted by denizens of the Web.

But to ensure that the same skeptics who now dismiss blockchain technology are wrong, entrepreneurs building Web3 startups will need to build tools that have real use cases, address a need, and demonstrate what decentralized tech can do.

Many are already doing it, applying blockchain to areas like decentralized data storage and video hosting, peer-to-peer payments, lightning-fast international remittances, faster and more private charitable donations, and fairer voting for group projects. But there are also many scams and fly-by-night money grabs – like in any new tech industry. To avoid the failures of the past (remember the ICO boom of 2018?) and to onboard the next million people into Web3, entrepreneurs in the space need to be honest, patient, strategic, and above all else, build products that matter.

—*Daniel Roberts, Editor in Chief of Decrypt*

Why Web3?

It's a Rethinking of the Internet

Since childhood, Gavin Wood has been interested in the convergence of economics and game theory.[1] He even co-published a board game of strategy. He was also an avid computer programmer, having started at age eight.

When Gavin became an adult, he worked at startups as well as Microsoft. His main focus was on leveraging computer visualizations and machine learning for music and audio systems.

In 2013, he met Vitalik Buterin, a programmer who wrote a paper about Ethereum, which was based on the emerging blockchain platform. Gavin was intrigued and coded the first workable client for it, which he referred to as PoC-1 (for "proof of concept"). He presented this at the North American Bitcoin Conference in January 2014.

---

[1] https://gavwood.com/

© Tom Taulli 2022
T. Taulli, *How to Create a Web3 Startup*,
https://doi.org/10.1007/978-1-4842-8683-8_1

Ethereum would quickly get adoption. But Gavin also saw this technology as the basis for a new type of Internet. He called it "Web3."[2] According to him: "This is [the] technology that is being used to build the new world — the world that's going to drive human civilization for the rest of this century, at least."[3] He then co-founded Polkadot, a technology startup, and the Web3 Foundation, a nonprofit organization that supports the category.

So, then what is Web3? Why has it received so much buzz? And why is it important for entrepreneurs? In this chapter, we'll take a look.

Definition of Web3

Web3 is still in the nascent stages. This means that the definition of this term is evolving. In a way, it's similar to what happened with the emergence of the Internet in the mid-1990s.

But let's take a look at a few definitions:

- The Web3 Glossary: "Web3 (noun, adjective) [is] the next iteration of the web being ushered in as we speak, which leverages blockchain technology, open-source applications, and the decentralization of data and information. Web3 aims to remove control of the web from monopolistic tech companies and return ownership of data and content to its users. Also referred to as the 'read-write-trust web.'"[4]

- Ethereum.org: "Web3, in the context of Ethereum, refers to decentralized apps that run on the blockchain. These are apps that allow anyone to participate without monetizing their personal data."[5]

---

[2] www.pcmag.com/how-to/what-is-web3-and-how-will-it-work#:~:text=The%20 term%20Web3%20was%20coined,being%20a%20decentralized%20digital%20 infrastructure

[3] https://cointelegraph.com/news/crypto-stories-gavin-wood-discusses-why-he-decided-to-code-ethereum

[4] https://unstoppabledomains.com/blog/the-web3-glossary

[5] https://ethereum.org/en/developers/docs/web2-vs-web3/#:~:text=Web3% 2C%20in%20the%20context%20of,without%20monetising%20their%20personal%20 data

- Digiday.com: "Web 3.0, or stylized as Web3, is the label being applied to a decentralized version of the internet that would be jointly owned by the users and the builders. Essentially, this is the antithesis to how centralized platforms like Apple, Google and Facebook operate, by monetizing data extracted from users on a daily basis."[6]

There are some common themes. First, Web3 rests on the blockchain stack of technologies. This means it is decentralized since users create the network and even own it. With it, they can engage in direct peer-to-peer interactions.

The fast-growing network is not controlled by a central entity, such as Facebook or Apple. In a sense, Web3 is a democratized version of the online world. Everyone owns their data and can monetize it themselves.

Now it's true that the Web2 Internet is based on a myriad of free protocols – and this is certainly a form of decentralization. But the reality is that – for most people – they need to use the large Internet providers to do anything meaningful, such as make connections, read or view content, and so on.

Web3 is also permissionless. This means that anyone can use it without having to create login credentials or get authorization from a central provider. When you are on the system, you cannot be kicked off.

Of course, all this only scratches the surface of Web3. But these concepts get to the high-level essence.

Note   The term Web3 has different variations. When Gavin Wood coined the term, he referred to it as Web 3.0. But it has also been called Web 3. Yet the general usage now is for Web3.

Web1

To better understand Web3, it is important to get a brief backgrounder on Web1 and Web2. No doubt, both of these periods were full of drama and rapid technological change. There was also a major impact on society.

Now the origins of Web1 go back to the late 1960s. The Internet was known as ARPANET, or the Advanced Research Projects Agency Network, and had the backing of the U.S. Department of Defense. At the core of this technology was packet switching, which allowed computers to communicate with each other. The idea was to have a network that could survive a nuclear war.

---

[6] https://digiday.com/media/wtf-is-web3/

However, ARPANET would be primarily for academic purposes. For example, the first online connection happened between research labs at UCLA and Stanford. Even though the message just had "Login," the system crashed anyway![7]

During the 1970s and 1980s, programmers developed a variety of protocols that were freely available. Some examples include Transmission Control Protocol and Internet Protocol, or TCP/IP, Domain name system (DNS), SMTP, or the Simple Message Transfer Protocol, and File Transfer Protocol (FTP). All these have remained critical for powering today's online world.

But in 1990, the Internet would change in a big way. Tim Berners-Lee created the World Wide Web, which allowed for hypertext links. For him, he thought this was a much better way for searching and reading academic papers.

But it would not take long until the Internet would become mainstream, allowing for searching and ecommerce. In 1993, college student Marc Andreessen helped to create the Mosaic web browser. From the start, it got huge numbers of downloads.

A year later, tech entrepreneur Jim Clark contacted Andreesen to build a company, called Netscape. The main product was the Navigator browser – and the growth was staggering. On August 9, 1995, Netscape came public at $28 a share and the price ended the day at $58.[8] The market valuation was $2.2 billion, even though the revenues for the past six months were only $16.6 million. There was a net loss of $4.31 million.

The IPO ignited the dot-com boom, which would last until 2000. Some interesting characteristics of this period include the following:

- Few people created content. Simply put, it was difficult to develop websites. You had to know HTML and scripting code. The dialup Internet connections made it challenging to use video and images.

- Creating startups was expensive and required the help of venture capitalists. You had to buy expensive servers and databases. It was also hard to find talent who could create the web technologies and there were not many useful development tools.

---

[7] www.history.com/news/who-invented-the-internet#:~:text=The%20first%20 workable%20prototype%20of,communicate%20on%20a%20single%20network
[8] www.nytimes.com/1995/08/10/us/with-internet-cachet-not-profit-a-new-stock-is-wall-st-s-darling.html

- A popular business model was advertising. This allowed for content sites like Yahoo! to provide their services for free. The ads were usually based on the number of views or "eyeballs."

- The Internet was still for a small part of the global population. By 2001, only about 50 million had access to broadband Internet.[9]

- Portals like Yahoo!, Lycos, Infoseek, AltaVista, and Excite became very important for the growth of Web1. They allowed many people to easily get useful information in one place.

According to Chris Dixon, a general partner at a16z: "Web1...was about open protocols that were decentralized and community governed. Most of the value accrued to the edges of the network — users and builders."[10]

The bottom line: It was very similar to the vision of Web3. Interestingly, a common notion is that Web3 is really a way to get back to the original principles of the Internet.

Yet this is likely an exaggeration. The fact is that Web1 saw centralization. And this was not necessarily a bad thing. It actually helped get a large number of people to participate in the ecosystem.

Part of this was due to the power of AOL, which was the Facebook of its era. AOL was like an alternative version of the Internet – and it held tremendous power. Because of its huge user base, the company was able to generate massive amounts of revenues from advertisements and sponsorships.

Then there was AOL's hugely popular chat system. It connected millions of users like a modern-day social network.

The Web1 world also highlighted something important that we've seen in Web2: The network effect. This is where a system gets more useful and powerful as more people join it.

A classic case of this was eBay. True, there were various other online auctions. But eBay quickly turned into the clear dominant platform because sellers were attracted to the large number of buyers and vice versa. In fact, today the company is still the leader in the space.

---

[9] www.wsj.com/articles/SB10001424053111903480904576512250915629460
[10] https://future.a16z.com/why-web3-matters/

Web2

The dot-com implosion was brutal. Many companies like Pets.com, Webvan, eToys, Go.com, and DrKoop.com simply ran out of money.

Venture capital dried up. Many people left Silicon Valley and went into other industries, like Wall Street. Everything seemed hopeless.

But the tech industry would rejuvenate itself and Web2 or Web 2.0 would emerge.

IT engineer, Dracy DiNucci, coined the term back in 1999 in an article entitled "Fragmented Future."[11] Her vision was that the Internet would become much more immersive and be prevalent across platforms outside of a computer, such as the TV, car dashboard, cell phone, and game machines.

But it was not until 2004 that Web 2.0 became part of the Silicon Valley buzz. For the most part, the concept was evolving from DiNucci's concept to where the Internet would be user centric. Anyone could create their own content and share it.

The leading companies in this era included Google, YouTube, Facebook, Snap, and Twitter. And yes, they remain very much relevant today. They are also exploring how to evolve in the Web3 world.

In 2006, Time Magazine chose Web 2.0 as the Person of the Year. The story noted that the Internet had "became a tool for bringing together the small contributions of millions of people and making them matter."[12] At the time, the red-hot property was MySpace.com. This social network allowed for users to create content and connect with friends.

The belief was that Web 2.0 was the beginning of a new egalitarian Internet. It was common to think of it as decentralized, since the users had the power.

But this would eventually fade. The mega operators like Google, Facebook, and Twitter would control much of the online world – including the valuable data on billions of people.

These companies would amass enormous power. Just look at Google. In the fourth quarter of 2021, the company posted revenues of $75 billion, up 32% on a year-over-year basis, and the profit was $20.6 billion.[13] The company had ten online properties with over 1 billion users.

---

[11] http://darcyd.com/fragmented_future.pdf
[12] www.oreilly.com/library/view/web-20-architectures/9780596514433/ch04s02.html#:~:text=Despite%20its%20being%20considered%20%E2%80%9Cso, Web%202.0%20was%20gathering%20steam
[13] https://abc.xyz/investor/static/pdf/2021Q4_alphabet_earnings_release. pdf?cache=d72fc76

The company also was more than search and online apps. It owned Waymo, one of the world's largest autonomous driving operators. It also controlled device companies like Fitbit and Nest.

So, was there too much power concentrated among too few companies? Many in the tech world believed that the answer was yes. And this was leading to major problems. After all, could a startup take on Google search? Or go after the Apple iPhone? Or dethrone Facebook's massive social network?

It would not be easy. The fight would also take huge amounts of resources.

As a result, the tech industry wanted to create a new paradigm – one that was truly decentralized and in control of the users. It was the Web3 paradigm.

"Web3 appeals to so many different kinds of people that have been slighted in one way or another by corrupted centralized parties," said Josh Neuroth, who is the head of product at Ankr. "Platforms like Facebook used and manipulated user data in ways we never thought possible. Governments failed citizens with economic policy, sanctions, hyperinflation. Now, people see ways to regain some privacy, autonomy, and freedom in Web3."[14]

■ **Note** Despite the criticism of Web2, there are definitely some key benefits. Keep in mind that centralization was necessary. The reason is that it would not have been possible to have enough scale to allow billions of people to become part of the online world. The advertising model was also key, as it meant much less friction for users to participate.

Catalysts for Web3

One of the biggest drivers for Web3 is definitely the threat of the megatech companies. But there are other factors at work. Here's a look:

- Composability: This is similar to an API (Application Programming Interface), which allows for Lego-like components to build programs and systems. In the Web3 context, composability uses the blockchain to evolve the applications – to build on each other. It's a way of "not reinventing the wheel."

---

[14] From the author's interview with Josh Neuroth on March 12, 2022.

- Need for a new platform: Today's Internet is similar to the one that existed in the early 1990s. But over time, there have emerged many new innovations. So shouldn't the foundation of the Internet better reflect this? Definitely. For Web3, this is essentially using blockchain as the core for a new architecture. But the platform will not just be limited to this. Web3 will also leverage other technologies like Virtual Reality (VR), Augmented Reality (AR), artificial intelligence (AI), IoT (Internet of Things) and 5G.

- FOMO (Fear of Missing Out): Yes, there are many entrepreneurs and investors who do not want to miss out on the next big thing.

- New business models: The monetization approaches for Web2 include advertising, subscriptions, and usage. But Web3 offers interesting new options. With the growth of cryptocurrencies and tokens, these may ultimately be the new way for monetizing the online world. Users will also essentially become the "shareholders" of the platform that they participate on. This could perhaps be the biggest motivator to get people to adopt Web3.

- Utopian Vision: Some influencers believe that Web3 will have a seismic impact on society. For example, Vitalik Buterin, who is the cofounder of Ethereum, believes that the technology will improve housing, voting, the distribution of goods, city planning, and even lifespans.

- Venture Funding: The interest has quickly reached fever levels. In 2021, venture funding in Web3 and crypto deals hit $27 billion.[15] This was more than the amounts raised during the prior ten years.

- The Metaverse: This is essentially a part of Web3. This is an immersive Internet, which involves VR and AR. Facebook CEO Mark Zuckerberg has bet his company on the Metaverse. He even changed the name of the company to Meta. In 2021, Zuckerberg spent $10 billion on his vision of the Metaverse – with a big focus on VR technologies.[16]

---

[15] www.nytimes.com/interactive/2022/03/18/technology/web3-definition-internet.html
[16] www.nytimes.com/2022/02/02/technology/meta-facebook-earnings-meta-verse.html

Microsoft was also looking to the Metaverse. To this end, the company agreed to pay $70 billion for Activision. "The metaverse is no small matter, with investors projecting that it could bring in $30 trillion in revenue over the next decade," said Marie Tatibouet, who is the CMO Of Gate.io. "The metaverse is part of the next evolution of the internet (Web 3.0) and has many avatars such as gaming, online communities, businesses, etc. It combines entertainment, traveling, business, and more with virtual reality and augmented reality, allowing users to live in a digital space. The metaverse marries both the physical and digital worlds."[17] However, with mega tech taking the lead in the development of the Metaverse, this is likely to lead to centralization. This could mean little choice and control of data for users.

In 2022, YouTube CEO Susan Wojcicki published a blog that set forth the video giant's priorities for 2022. And yes, Web3 was a major theme:

> We're also looking further ahead to the future and have been following everything happening in Web3 as a source of inspiration to continue innovating on YouTube. The past year in the world of crypto, nonfungible tokens (NFTs), and even decentralized autonomous organizations (DAOs) have highlighted a previously unimaginable opportunity to grow the connection between creators and their fans. We're always focused on expanding the YouTube ecosystem to help creators capitalize on emerging technologies, including things like NFTs, while continuing to strengthen and enhance the experiences creators and fans have on YouTube.

Ironically, when this letter was published, several of YouTube's executives departed for Web3 startups.

---

[17] From the author's interview with Marie Tatibouet on March 18, 2022.

Web3 and Crypto

When Russia invaded Ukraine in early 2022, the values of cryptocurrencies surged. Part of this was due to people looking for safe havens for their wealth. But people were also using cryptocurrencies to help the people in Ukraine. Within a few weeks, there were over $64 million in donations, according to blockchain analytics firm Elliptic.[18]

But there was a dark side to this as well. It looked like cryptocurrencies were helping Russia avoid some of the sanctions. They could also be a way for oligarchs to hide their assets. Because of this, Massachusetts Senator Elizabeth Warren introduced legislation to deal with these issues. She noted that – in 2021 – close to three-quarters of all ransomware was due to Russian-linked entities.[19]

Note that this controversy with cryptocurrencies and blockchain was nothing new. It began in the early days of these systems and technologies. For example, it was common for tax evaders, drug traffickers, human traffickers, and hackers to use cryptocurrencies and blockchain to bolster their illicit activities. Unfortunately, these remain problems today.

As a result, Web3 may actually be an attempt to essentially rebrand cryptocurrencies and blockchain. It is a way to make it more of a normal technology. Besides, if Web3 takes off, this will also mean much more demand for crypto.

Note   Larry Fink is the CEO of BlackRock, which is an asset management firm that has about $10 trillion in assets. He believes that the Russian-Ukraine war will accelerate the adoption of crypto. In his annual shareholder letter, he wrote: "The war will prompt countries to re-evaluate their currency dependencies. Even before the war, several governments were looking to play a more active role in digital currencies and define the regulatory frameworks under which they operate."[20] If so, this will likely be a major positive for Web3, which relies heavily on crypto.

---

[18] www.barrons.com/articles/russia-ukraine-war-cryptocurrencies-51647548970
[19] www.barrons.com/advisor/articles/crypto-regulation-russia-sanctions-elizabeth-warren-51646427551
[20] www.cnbc.com/2022/03/24/blackrocks-fink-says-russia-ukraine-war-could-accelerate-use-of-cryptocurrencies.html

The Downsides of Web3

Web3 is far from a no-brainer. Let's face it, history has shown that there have been many emerging technologies that never hit critical mass. Here's a look at some famous examples:

- Segway: Launched in 2001, this was a motorized scooter with two wheels on the side. The driver guided it by leaning. John Doer, the famed venture capitalist, said that the Segway had the potential to be bigger than the Internet.[21] Well, unfortunately, it was a major flop. The Segway would become the object of jokes.

- Speech Recognition: In late 1997, Bill Gates said: "The PC five years from now — you won't recognize it, because speech will have come into the interface, the screen will be a flat screen, the performance will be 20 times what it is today."[22] He was far off the mark with speech recognition. The fact is that this technology was incredibly challenging to develop. It really wasn't until the great strides in deep learning – from 2012 or so – that speech recognition became useful to users.

OK then, so when it comes to Web3, what are the nagging issues? How might this technology not live up to the expectations? Could it even just be another fad?

Here are some factors to consider:

- Performance: So far, it is not very impressive. Blockchain networks are generally slow and have high transaction costs. Consider that they are a big user of energy. In 2021, Bitcoin transactions consumed about 91 terawatt-hours of electricity. This was more than the usage for Finland.[23] The reason is that Bitcoin transaction involve solving complex mathematical problems, which take up enormous amounts of compute power.

---

[21] http://content.time.com/time/business/article/0,8599,186660,00.html
[22] https://doanchienthangenglish.wordpress.com/2006/05/05/6/
[23] www.nytimes.com/interactive/2021/09/03/climate/bitcoin-carbon-foot-print-electricity.html

- User Experience: For the most part, it is fairly difficult to use Web3 systems. The interfaces are often not intuitive, and you may need a technical background. The jargon and concepts of Web3 can quickly get complicated, such as with the use of dApps. This will make it difficult to get mainstream adoption.

- Bubble: There has already been intense interest from VCs drove. The result can be a bubble that ultimately pops. For Web1, this happened from 1996 to 2000. And perhaps the same could happen with Web3. Although, bubbles are not necessarily bad either. They are common when there is a massively disruptive technology.

- Dystopia: The world of Web3 may turn out to be worse than Web2. After all, many of the transactions will have some type of payment mechanism – and it may not be clear how viable the tokens will ultimately be. There could also be lots of fragmentation, with people focusing on micro platforms. Something else: Web3 will track everything and make the transactions public. But many people may value privacy more.

- Centralization: When you look at the history of technology, there is a similar pattern. First, there are new innovations that emerge, and this attracts a growing number of people. They create their own startups to capitalize on the opportunity. Many will ultimately fail or be purchased. And yes, the result will be centralization. This was the case with megatrends like mainframes in the 1950s and 1960s, and the PC and software in the 1980s and 1990. So why will Web3 be any different? It very well may not. Besides, the current incumbents like Facebook, Apple, and Google have tremendous power – and will certainly wield it to protect their global platforms.

Another lingering issue with Web3 is that it is male dominated. It's actually kind of a proverbial bro culture.

This will definitely need to change. For Web3 to be successful, there must be true diversity.

Now there are some encouraging signs of change. Just look at Katie Haun. From 2006 to 2017, she served as a federal prosecutor, and she focused on cyber and crypto crimes.[24] She created the first federal cryptocurrency task force, which investigated the Mt. Gox hack and the criminals on the Silk Road network.

After this, she moved to the private sector and became a general partner at Andreessen Horowitz.[25] At the firm, she led investments in breakout crypto companies. She would also go on to serve on various boards, such as for Coinbase.

In early 2022, she raised $1.5 billion for two funds for crypto and Web3.[26] In aggregate, they were the largest ever with a female general partner.

In a blog post announcing the new venture fund, she wrote:

> The web3 projects that emerge over the next decade will be even more expansive, applying the breakthrough mechanisms of the last decade to every industry from transportation and commerce to fashion, sports, music, and more. We think consumer demand for digitally native experiences and goods will continue to increase. As more people embrace these products, there will be a shift in individuals' expectations for greater control of their personal data and a new generation of creators will demand and enjoy better economics. We think open platforms will win through loyalty, transparency, and trust by delivering better incentives than the walled gardens that came before.[27]

The Billionaire Web3 Spat

In late December 2021, Jack Dorsey departed as the CEO of Twitter and then changed the name of the other company he served as CEO: Square. He renamed the firm "Block." This was because of his fervent belief in the power of blockchain and crypto. He noted: "I don't think there's anything more important in my lifetime to work on."[28]

---

[24] www.linkedin.com/in/kathryn-haun-0791456/details/experience/
[25] https://a16z.com/author/katie-haun/
[26] www.wsj.com/articles/katie-hauns-crypto-venture-capital-funds-break-records-11648068381?mod=hp_lista_pos4
[27] https://mirror.xyz/haunventures.eth/XHOD9o8ZjALuf7QnJz-oydihpROmtOtxDFYIMOUoUzY
[28] www.wsj.com/articles/square-changes-name-to-block-days-after-ceo-jack-dorsey-leaves-twitter-11638394200

At the time, Block had roughly $220 million in bitcoin on its balance sheet. On Dorsey's Twitter bio, it just had one hashtag: #bitcoin.

Then what about his opinion about Web3? Interestingly enough, he is not so sanguine. He tweeted: "You don't own 'web3.' The VCs and their LPs do. It will never escape their incentives. It's ultimately a centralized entity with a different label. Know what you're getting into..."[29]

This was certainly provocative. It was a direct hit against one of the central themes of Web3.

The tweet sparked reactions from other tech billionaires. For example, Elon Musk tweeted: "Has anyone seen web3? I can't find it."[30]

Dorsey was quick to respond to this. His tweet was: "somewhere between a and z." No doubt, this was a clear shot at venture firm, Andreessen Horowitz, one of the largest investors in crypto and Web3. The firm is often referred to as "A16Z."

Things got so heated that Marc Andreessen would block Dorsey on Twitter. Dorsey then tweeted: "I'm officially banned from Web3."[31]

It is really too early to see who will be right. However, it seems inevitable that VCs will be critical to the growth of Web3. They will not only provide much-needed capital to build the infrastructure and scale the systems, but they will be helpful in providing strategic advice.

For entrepreneurs, having venture funding will likely be a key ingredient – even if it may ultimately dampen one of the Web3 ideals of decentralization.

"There will likely always be centralized systems or components within the web, and that is okay," said Josh Neuroth, who is the head of product at Ankr. "But Web3 is about getting the communities engaged and decentralizing power, not always the systems themselves."[32]

■ **Note** In late December 2021, Elon Musk tweeted: "I'm not suggesting web3 is real – seems more marketing buzzword than reality right now – just wondering what the future will be like in 10, 20 or 30 years. 2051 sounds crazy futuristic!"[33]

---

[29] https://bit.ly/3NnRNme
[30] https://twitter.com/elonmusk/status/1473165434518224896?lang=en
[31] www.cnbc.com/2021/12/23/jack-dorsey-blocked-by-marc-andreessen-on-twitter-after-web3-comments.html
[32] From the author's interview with Josh Neuroth on March 12, 2022.
[33] https://twitter.com/elonmusk/status/1472745072277995526?s=20

The Web3 Platform Shift

In the history of technology, there have been various platform shifts. This is when there is a disruptive change in the core layer. This is what happened when the mainframe industry transitioned to minicomputers. Then, minicomputers would transition to the PC industry.

When this happens, the incumbents often suffer. They have to cannibalize their existing businesses to make the changes. But often there is little change. For example, many of the leaders during the 1980s in the PC software industry would lose their positions in the 1990s. This was because the platform changed from DOS-based applications to the Windows platform. The result is that companies like Borland, WordPerfect, Novell, and Lotus came under tremendous pressure. Of course, Microsoft would benefit from the changes since it controlled Windows. But there were many new entrants that came to the market.

As for Web3, this could represent a massive platform change – and it is likely to last for many years. According to Sequoia partner, Michelle Bailhe, the firm's conviction is that "crypto is one of the most important platform shifts of our time."[34]

This means there are huge opportunities for entrepreneurs to create innovations and build the new ecosystem.

The Startup

What are the keys to the success of a Web3 startup? Interestingly enough, much of it will be the same for any startup. For example, look at the founding of Microsoft in 1975. Here were some of the key factors:

- Team: While Bill Gates and Paul Allen were young, they actually had lots of experience with computers. True, they were mainframes. But Gates and Allen learned the core fundamentals of the technology and liked to experiment with new approaches. They would also recruit very smart developers – which helped to accelerate the growth. This, in turn, would attract more and more developers.

---

[34] www.sequoiacap.com/article/ask-not-wen-moon-ask-why-moon/

- Strategic Vision: Gates and Allen knew that the PC would revolutionize the world. It would impact businesses, the home, everything. They also understood that software would be the key value driver.

- Market Size: The mission statement for Microsoft was simple yet powerful: "a computer on every desk and in every home." In other words, Gates and Allen were thinking very big. They saw that the market was enormous, and that Microsoft would be the clear leader.

- Platform: Microsoft was not just a set of different tools. Rather, it was a platform. In the 1980s, this was based on DOS, which was the dominant operating system. It became a significant cash generator. Gates and Allen then parlayed this into building the next OS, which was Windows. They always looked at their technology strategically.

- Partnerships: As a small company in the early days, Microsoft did not have many resources. But it was able to leverage the power of partnerships. The main one was with IBM. Microsoft would become the default OS for its PC.

The preceding will definitely be part of most successful Web3 startups. But then, what is different? Well, it really comes down to understanding the major trends and the customer needs. These feed into the strategic vision, market size, and partnership opportunities. In fact, success can easily come down to making a few right choices.

To continue with the Microsoft example, the company could have easily become a footnote in technology history. The reason is that – when IBM came to the company – it did not have an operating system. Instead, the dominant player in this category was Digital Research, which had CP/M. Funny enough, Gates recommended that IBM visit the company. However, the CEO of Digital Research was skeptical. So Gates saw an opportunity and purchased QDOS (which stood for "quick and dirty operating system") from Seattle Computer Systems on July 27, 1981 for $50,000.[35] This would become the core technology for MS-DOS and lead to billions of dollars in revenues.

---

[35] www.windowscentral.com/microsoft-bought-ms-dos-os-early-ibm-pcs-july-27-1981

Conclusion

Again, Web3 is still in the early innings. It will take years for there to be clear-cut themes and breakout applications. This should not be a surprise. It's the case with any major shift in technology.

But for Web3, it is generally about decentralization of the platform, which is powered by blockchain and crypto. There will also be new management structures and business models. Then there will be a need to improve the performance of the underlying blockchain technology as well as to build a new type of infrastructure. Oh, and the user experiences need to be simpler and much less technical. There will also need to be more diversity. All in all, this means Web3 will offer more than enough great opportunities for entrepreneurs.

There are some Web3 influencers who believe that this new approach will revolutionize the world – and it will be mostly a good thing. But while there will certainly be many positives, there will be problems too. Yet again, this means more opportunities for entrepreneurs. Building the Web3 world will take patience and lots of hard work.

A successful Web3 startup will have many of the same qualities of any tech startup. There will need to be a strong team, the solving of tough problems, and a large market opportunity. However, in the context of Web3, entrepreneurs will differentiate themselves by understanding the pathways of the technology.

So, in the next chapter, we'll look at the core tech stack, which includes blockchain and Ethereum.

Core Technology

Blockchain, Ethereum, and Other Platforms

Besides running highly successful companies like SpaceX and Tesla, Elon Musk somehow has time to focus on the cryptocurrency world. This is definitely apparent from his Twitter feed. Oh, and of course, during early 2022, he bought 9% of the company and attempted a takeover!

Some of his tweets are comical – but the world pays close attention. When Musk posted a shiba inu puppy image on Twitter, the altcoin called shiba inu spiked. He also had a major impact on dogecoin. This is a cryptocurrency that actually started as a joke.

Here's what he tweeted about it: "Lots of people I talked to on the production lines at Tesla or building rockets at SpaceX own Doge. They aren't financial experts or Silicon Valley technologists. That's why I decided to support Doge – it felt like the people's crypto."[1]

---

[1] https://twitter.com/elonmusk/status/1452348126753349640

© Tom Taulli 2022
T. Taulli, *How to Create a Web3 Startup*,
https://doi.org/10.1007/978-1-4842-8683-8_2

In May 2021, Musk was the guest host on Saturday Night Live and his performance garnered mixed reviews. But he did mention dogecoin, saying it was a "hustle."[2] The price of the cryptocurrency plunged nearly 30%.

No doubt, the crypto world is wild and volatile. But it is becoming mainstream. And Musk is one of the main influencers. Although, this certainly has its downsides. Musk is facing lawsuits, such as for his alleged manipulation of dogecoin. Tesla also sold a large amount of its Bitcoin holdings.

Regardless, the core blockchain technology for crypto is relatively new. There continues to be much evolution and change. Thus, for entrepreneurs looking at Web3, you need to have a solid understanding of the core blockchain technology. You will also need to keep up with some of the emerging alternative platforms.

In this chapter, we'll get an overview of them.

The Origins of Blockchain

To understand blockchain, it is important to get an overview of some of the major technology developments that led to its creation. This will provide context and an understanding of why blockchain is so powerful and unique.

First of all, you need a backgrounder on databases. They were a critical technology in the early days of mainframe computers. They allowed for storing, accessing, deleting, and updating information. They were essential for managing applications, such as handling a company's payroll or calculating the rocket paths for the Apollo program.

It was during the 1970s that the database technology saw a major innovation. This was the relational database. It was based on storing information in tables – which had columns and rows of data – that you could use a relatively easy language, SQL (Structured Query Language), for managing them. IBM researcher E. F. Codd invented this technology. But interestingly enough, his employer was lukewarm on its potential. The belief was that relational databases could not scale for large enterprises. Although, the main reason may have been that IBM did not want to cannibalize its existing database business, such as for IMS.

Computer engineer Larry Ellison read Codd's work and was intrigued. He believed that this was the future of the database industry. To capitalize on this opportunity, he cofounded Oracle. True, IBM would eventually launch its own relational database, Db2, but it was really too late. Oracle would ultimately become the dominant player in the market.

---

[2] www.cnbc.com/2021/05/08/dogecoin-price-plummets-as-elon-musk-hosts-saturday-night-live-.html#:~:text=As%20Elon%20Musk%20%E2%80%93%20the%20self,%2C%E2%80%9D%20SNL's%20satirical%20news%20show

What's interesting is that relational databases have not seen much innovation. As a result, startups have taken advantage of this. During the past decade, there have emerged new technologies like NoSQL. Some of the companies in the space have become fast-growth operators, such as MongoDb.

But despite this, databases have certain limitations. They generally rely on administrators. They have certain authorizations and rights to use features and capabilities of the databases. While this usually works, there can be problems. There can be errors or hacks. Or an administrator may even perpetuate the breach.

There are various types of security systems like firewalls. But they are far from foolproof.

But this is where blockchain becomes very intriguing. It is a database – but it is distributed. This means that everyone on the network has access to it. They can see every transaction since inception. There is also no administrator of the database. Instead, the management is based on the efforts of everyone in the network. It is truly decentralized.

There are three main components to this system:

- Blocks: There are a chain of these, and each block holds data, such as for a currency transaction. When you make a block, the system will make a 32-bit number called a nonce. This is used to generate a block header– and this is a 256-bit number. It is part of the cryptography to allow for securing the data on the blockchain.

- Nodes: These are the computers on the blockchain network. The decisions for the network are based on the collective actions of the nodes. They are not the result of a central authority. Instead, nodes will verify where a new block is trusted and verified. They have another advantage – that is, durability. If a few nodes fail, the system will continue to work. By contrast, this would not be the case for a traditional database in a data center.

- Miners: With computers, it is easy to copy huge amounts of data. But the blockchain prohibits this. To create new blocks, you need miners. They use sophisticated algorithms to solve math problems to make the nonces that have the right hashes. Some of the ways to achieve this include proof of work (PoW) or proof of stake (PoS). However, it gets more difficult to solve the problem as the network grows because the calculations need to account for all the blocks. When a miner finds the right combination, it is called the golden nonce. The result is that it is very difficult to hack the blockchain. It would require that a majority of the nodes agree to change the blocks to carry out a fraud.

Something else: When a transaction is created, it cannot be changed. This is another form of security.

Over the years, blockchain has proven quite resilient. But the first main test of this technology was Bitcoin.

■ **Note**   During the early days of crypto, you could use your home PC to mine coins. But those days are over. Mining is now done with the use of highly sophisticated computers, such as GPUs (Graphics Processing Units). They are known as "mining rigs." In fact, there are a variety of publicly traded companies that operate mining businesses, such as Marathon Digital Holdings and Riot Blockchain.

Bitcoin

The origins of cryptocurrencies go back to the late 1970s. Academics looked at approaches to create a digital monetary unit based on complex cryptography.

For example, in 1979, doctorate student Ralph Merkle wrote his dissertation about the use of public keys and digital signatures to verify transactions. This became known as the Merkle tree.

Then, by the early 1990s, professors Stuart Haber and W. Scott Stornetta released a paper about how to prevent the manipulation of digital transactions. To help with this, they used Merkle trees.

With this academic research, entrepreneurs started to test the theories. One was David Chaum. He developed a technology that used public and private key systems for digital signatures. He then founded a company, DigiCash, in 1990 to prove his concepts. It relied on the transactions of traditional banks. However, the information about the parties were private. Unfortunately, Chaum could only get a handful of banks interested in the technology and DigiCash would file for bankruptcy in 2002.

During the 1990s, there were other interesting startups that created cryptocurrencies. Examples included Flooz, Bit Gold, and Hashcash. But they would all eventually fail.

By 2008, the situation would prove ideal for the creation of a sustainable cryptocurrency. With the financial crisis, many people were losing trust in the government and financial services companies. Maybe a digital alternative would be better?

Well, Satoshi Nakamoto wrote a pivotal paper. It was called "Bitcoin: A Peer-to-Peer Electronic Cash System."

Keep in mind that the identity of Nakamoto was not disclosed. He or she may have been one person or a group of persons. But it did not matter. What was important is that Nakamoto's paper ignited a revolution. Nakamoto provided the basis for the blockchain framework and tested it with the creation of the first sustainable cryptocurrency.

On January 3, 2009, Nakamoto mined the first bitcoin block. This indicated the validity of the technology. For the first transaction, there were 50 bitcoins created – and they have since been called the "Genesis block" or block 0.

Nakamoto then made the Bitcoin software open source. This meant that it was freely available for anyone to download from the Internet. It also allowed any programmer to make changes to the code.

Next, on January 12, 2009, Nakamoto executed the first Bitcoin transaction. He sent block 170 – which had 10 bitcoin – to Hal Finney. The address of the transaction was the public key, which was a long string of numbers. For Hal to access and own it, he had his own private key. Think of this as a complex password.

Note that the transaction involved no intermediaries. There was no bank or government authority to process the transaction and charge a fee. The Bitcoin was sent peer-to-peer and the blockchain handled everything. This meant it was a true decentralized system.

In other words, Bitcoin was instantly global. All you needed was access to the Internet. The network was always open. You could send Bitcoin to someone at midnight on Sunday. It did not matter.

The Bitcoin transaction did not require any personal information, like a Social Security number, address, or even a name. There was only the use of the public and private keys. This meant there was no chance for identity fraud or hacking private information.

Finally, the Bitcoin transaction was added to the public blockchain ledger. This was similar to what a bank would have – except that everyone on the network could see it.

Note   In the Bitcoin code, there is halving. This means that – every four years – the amount of new coins gets reduced by 50%. The next halving will occur in May 2024.

Then did Bitcoin have the characteristics of a true currency? Granted, it was not a fiat currency. This is where a government issues the currency and it is not backed by a physical commodity, like gold or silver. For example, in the USA, the dollar is backed by the "full faith and credit" of the government.

A cryptocurrency also does not have a physical form. There are no paper versions.

But Bitcoin certainly has other aspects of a currency. They include the following:

- Divisibility: This means you can divide the currency into other denominations. For example, you can exchange a 10-dollar bill for 10 one-dollar bills or two 5-dollar bills. Interestingly enough, Bitcoin is more divisible than the dollar. One bitcoin is divided up to eight decimal places and each is called a Satoshi.

- Limited Supply: If the government prints too many dollars, then there will be inflation or even hyperinflation. Eventually, people will not accept it because the currency will be worthless. However, in the case of Bitcoin, it has a programmed limit – that is, 21 million units. There are about 19 million in existence today. The estimate is that it will take until 2140 for the 21 million limit to be reached.

- Uniformity: A currency needs to be interchangeable. For example, a $10 bill is worth the same as any other one. Then what about Bitcoin? It is uniform as well. The main reason is that the blockchain verification system allows for authenticating each of the transactions.

- Portability: You can easily transfer the currency. And yes, this is definitely true with Bitcoin. You can send it to anyone on the network. Like the US dollar, you do not have to use any personal information for a transaction.

- Durability: This is where the currency can deteriorate or be destroyed. An example would be US dollars that are burned and can no longer be retrieved. With Bitcoin, everything is on the network. So long as this is maintained, there will be durability.

- Acceptability: This means that you can use a currency for many transactions. But for Bitcoin, this is far from the case. The fact is there are only a limited number of places – such as retail or ecommerce platforms – that you can use the cryptocurrency.

While bitcoin has many of the characteristics of a currency, it is still more of a store-of-value or an investment vehicle. It's become more like a stock or bond. In fact, this is what the IRS considers it to be. And this can cause many complex tax problems. Suppose you buy one bitcoin for $20,000 and it increases to $30,000. You then use this coin to buy a car in the USA. In this situation, you would owe taxes on the $10,000 gain. This would not have been the case if you used the US dollar.

Another problem with Bitcoin as a currency is the volatility. This makes it extremely difficult for businesses to do adequate planning. Let's say an automotive manufacturer accepts Bitcoin for its vehicles. During the first quarter, it sells 200,000 units at an average of $40,000 each. However, during the second quarter, Bitcoin plunges by 50%. In other words, the car company will report a steep drop in sales – and probably a net loss – even though it may have sold a higher number of cars.

Of course, there are various Bitcoin billionaires. They had the foresight or luck to buy up the cryptocurrency in the early years. In 2010, you could have purchased a Bitcoin for a fraction of a cent. As of 2022, it was fetching over $60,000.

Note   In 2013, Laszlo Hanyecz offered anyone 10,000 bitcoins to deliver two Papa John's pizzas to him. Someone took him up on this and it represented the first real-world Bitcoin transaction. But in hindsight, it was a bad move for Hanyecz. Had he kept his Bitcoin instead, they would have been worth over $300 million.[3]

Crypto Exchanges

While the blockchain allowed for a highly secure system, it was far from convenient. In the early days, if you wanted to create a transaction with Bitcoin, you would need to download and use complex software.

But entrepreneurs saw this as an opportunity to create new applications. A big part of this was the development of crypto exchanges. The first one came in 2010: Bitcoin Market. This allowed for the purchase of the cryptocurrency by using PayPal and an escrow system.

No doubt, many other exchanges would soon hit the markets. Examples included Mt. Gox and Tradehill, which allowed for instant purchases.

In 2011, the market would face a severe test – and the Bitcoin market nearly self-destructed. The reason was the hack of the Mt. Gox marketplace. It resulted in the collapse of the price of Bitcoin, which hit nearly $0. Suddenly, there was little trust in cryptocurrencies.

---

[3] www.yahoo.com/now/bitcoin-pizza-day-sees-first-112000121. html#:~:text=2010%2C%20Florida%20Man%20Laszlo%20Hanyecz,transaction%20 with%20an%20actual%20company

Despite all this, Mt. Gox was able to recover in a few years. The exchange also became the global leader.

Yet the problems would remain for the crypto industry. The US Department of Homeland Security engaged in several investigations and ordered some exchanges to change their practices.

Oh, and the issues with Mt. Gox were far from over. In 2014, the exchange had problems with settling trades. Then there was a bombshell announcement: a hack of over 850,000 Bitcoin.[4] While Mt. Gox recovered 200,000 of these, it was certainly not enough. The exchange would file for bankruptcy.

Over the years, there would be other hacks of crypto exchanges. Just some included Bithumb, ShapeShift, and Bitfinex.

Yet the Bitcoin market continued to be resilient. Then again, the early adopters had a high tolerance for risk. They were also big believers in the cryptocurrencies.

But to get mainstream acceptance, the "wild west" ways could not continue. As a result, the industry moved toward more compliance, such as with the adoption of anti-money laundering and counterterrorism financing requirements.

For example, in April 2021, Coinbase became the first crypto exchange in the United States to go public. The initial public offering price was $250, and the shares ended the day at $328.28, bringing the market capitalization to $85.8 billion.[5] Not bad for a company that was founded in 2012.

The growth of the company was staggering. During the first quarter, the revenues hit $1.8 billion, up 9X over the past year. The company's net income soared from $32 million to $730 million–$800 million. There were 6.1 million monthly transacting users (MTUs).

Crypto Wallets

When you buy a cryptocurrency, you need a place to store it. This is done with a digital wallet. There are two types available:

- Hot Wallet: This is where you store the cryptocurrency on the exchange. This is definitely easy. However, there can be risks if the exchange has troubles. After all, there

---

[4] www.abi.org/feed-item/bankrupt-bitcoin-exchange-mt-gox-begins-to-pay-back-account-holders-in-bitcoin
[5] www.cnbc.com/2021/04/14/coinbase-to-debut-on-nasdaq-in-direct-listing.html

is no equivalent of a Federal Deposit Insurance Corporation (FDIC) to back any lost cryptocurrency, as is the case with your deposits at a traditional bank.

- Cold Wallet: This is a physical device like a thumb drive. This is quite safe since there is little connection to the Internet. Then again, a cold wallet can make it more difficult for conducting transactions. Some of the common ones include CoolWallet Pro, Safepal S1, and Trezor Model T. The prices range from $50 to $150 or so.

Altcoins

In 2011, a variation of Bitcoin hit the markets. It was called Namecoin. It became part of a category of cryptocurrencies called altcoins. Basically, this meant something that was not Bitcoin.

The open-source platform allowed for altcoins. For the most part, they were ways to add new capabilities and innovations. In the case of Namecoin, it allowed for merged mining. This meant that a miner could mine more than one blockchain at the same time.

Over the years, there have been many new altcoins created. There are currently over 17,000.[6]

Yet Bitcoin remains the dominant cryptocurrency and ether as No. 2. They account for a majority of the world's transactions.

With so many altcoins, how can one analyze them? One way has been to divide them into different categories. Here are the main ones:

- Stablecoins: This is an altcoin whose value is connected to another asset. This may be a fiat currency, gold or anything else of value. The goal of a stablecoin is to provide stability. Essentially, it can perform the function of a traditional currency. A popular stablecoin is Tether and its value is tied to the US dollar. It was actually the first one created. However, in May 2022, various stablecoins plunged in value.[7] It was essentially a "run on the bank." Some of the stablecoins dropped more than 90% in a few days.

---

[6] https://time.com/nextadvisor/investing/cryptocurrency/altcoins/
[7] www.wsj.com/articles/cryptocurrency-terrausd-plunges-as-investors-bail-11652256429?mod=hp_lead_pos1

- Governance Token: This is an altcoin that provides a mechanism for voting on a blockchain project. This type of token is what is often used for DeFi (Decentralized Finance) and gaming systems. Some of the issues you can vote on include charging and setting fees, making changes to the interface of a network, or transferring funds to members. Also, there is no mining of governance tokens. They are distributed based on those who invest in the project. It's similar to being a shareholder in a company.

- Memecoins: These are altcoins that are more about fun and entertainment. Interestingly, some of them started as mere jokes. Regardless, memecoins can potentially have lots of value. But it can be tough to sustain this. Let's face it, there is usually something else new to take its place. Memecoins are more about fads.

- Utility Tokens: These are altcoins often used for online services. They are also common for Web3 applications. The most popular of the utility tokens is Ether, which has a "gas fee." This is for the cost of data processing. Another widely used utility token is Filecoin. With this, you can buy storage on the blockchain.

- Security Tokens: These allow you to acquire interests like real estate or artwork. The ownership can also be fractional.

Whenever there is a change in the blockchain protocol – such as with the creation of new rules or altcoins – there is a fork. This means there is a split in the network. And the new blockchain will have its own ledger.

There are two types of forks:

- Soft Fork: This is essentially an upgrade to the existing blockchain, and the network's users must approve it. There also needs to be backwards compatibility with the existing forks.

- Hard fork: This is where there is a clear split and there is no longer backwards compatibility. This is when there will often be the creation of a new cryptocurrency.

The Value of Cryptocurrency

Cryptocurrencies can definitely be risky. For Bitcoin, it's not uncommon for there to be jumps or drops of 20%.

Then how do you value a cryptocurrency? There are no clear-cut rules. It's not like a traditional asset like a stock. With this, the valuation is generally based on the profits of the company and the growth prospects.

Despite all this, there are still some factors to consider with valuing cryptocurrencies, including the following:

- Hedge: Some people invest in cryptocurrencies just to have some exposure to the asset. It's a way to get diversification but also to not miss out on potential returns.

- Scarcity: Many cryptocurrencies have limits on how many coins can be issued. This can make the digital asset scarce. So when demand rises, there can be significant increases in the price.

- Influencers: As we've seen earlier in this chapter, people like Elon Musk can have a huge impact on the prices of cryptocurrencies – and this could be a matter of a single tweet.

- Adoption: Traditional financial services companies like banks have been investing in cryptocurrencies and blockchain. This provides validation and demand.

- Hacks: From time to time, there are high-profile ones. The result is that there can be disruption in the crypto markets.

- Regulations: Governments tend to be slow with new restrictions. But whenever there are actions, there can be notable impacts on the valuations.

- Immature Market: Cryptocurrencies are still in the early stages. Unlike stocks or bonds, there is not a long history of performance during periods of war, inflation, recessions, depressions, and so on.

Ethereum

Ethereum has several use cases. One is for allowing transactions of a cryptocurrency. The coin is referred to as ETH or ether. In early 2022, the price was about $3,400 and the total value of the market was $412 billion.

Another important use case – especially for Web3 – is that Ethereum allows you to create smart contracts. Essentially, this means you can create programs on the blockchain.

For the crypto world, this was revolutionary. Ethereum was not just about creating a new cryptocurrency. You could create any type of application. This could be for financial services, legal services or even a cool game. It's only a matter of your imagination.

A key to smart contracts is the triggering of events based on certain conditions that are a part of an agreement between users. This is about traditional programming structures of If/then else statements. For example, an Ethereum smart contract may release funds if a party performs a service.

Now this can get complicated, such as in terms of the workflows. You want to game out the scenarios with the applications. If not, there could be actions taken that may result in a financial loss or a bad customer experience. There should also be a system of rules for resolving disputes.

To make an Ethereum transaction, you need to setup an account and there are two types. First, there are Externally Owned Accounts (EOA). This is where you have control with a private key and there is no code with it. You can send ether or messages from this account.

Next, there is the Contract account, which has its own code that is triggered when there is a transaction from an EOA. This type of account cannot initiate transactions. They can only come when there is a transaction from an EOA.

But there are usually few credentials you need to provide to open either account. You then spend Ether for a transaction. One of the reasons for this is to prohibit users – or even hackers – from bombarding the network with needless transactions. Next, the ether is a way to reward miners for validating transactions and providing compute resources to the network.

As mentioned earlier, the fee for using the Ethereum network is based on a unit called gas. And yes, you pay this with Ether, and they have dominations called gwei. Consider that there is 1 Ether for 1,000,000,000 gwei.

Like a typical blockchain, a smart contract makes it possible for users to transact with each other without the need for a trusted intermediary. The system is decentralized. There is also a copy of the ledger for everyone to see.

Here are other benefits of Ethereum:

- Agility: When you execute a contract, it is done instantly. There is nothing to fill out. There is also no need to reconcile errors.

- Security: This is at a high level because of the use of encryption.

- Backup: All smart contracts are stored many times on the blockchain. This means you will not have data loss.

- Maturity: As the first system for smart contracts, there is the advantage of a refined set of features. There is also a large number of developers. This means that – if you have a question – you probably will get an answer from the community.

- Standard: Ethereum has become the most common blockchain for DeFi and NFTs. This means that a large amount of value is locked in the blockchain. "The main pro for Ethereum is its enormous adoption and wide audience of users," said Alex Melikhov, who is the CEO and founder of Equilibrium. "If you deploy your application on Ethereum, you have potential access to a large-scale audience of users who are already familiar with blockchain technology and its infrastructure. They will not struggle with basic things like setting up a wallet or sending transactions but will be able to start using your application right away."

Each smart contract is stored on an address of the blockchain. This is contract address. Note that the developer does not come up with this. Instead, the contract address is based on a complex hash function calculation.

In terms of the development of smart contracts, you can use a variety of languages. Some of the common ones include Solidity and Vyper.

You will then need to compile the programs using the Ethereum Virtual Machine (EVM). This translates the code into bytecode and then is put on the blockchain.

Now this is different than a typical development environment – and the reason is the blockchain. For example, when a smart contract is executed, all the nodes on the network carry it out too. This is done with the EVM. This is all part of the process of verifying and accepting the smart contract.

The smart contract transaction will have a gas limit. If the processing results in a higher amount, then the transaction will not be completed on the network. But the sender of the of Ether for the smart contract will be reimbursed.

Then what are the downsides of Ethereum? Let's take a look:

- Scalability: This has proven to be perhaps the biggest problem. "The transactions are not scalable, and its users also have to pay high transaction fees per transaction," said Pratik Gandhi, who is the Head of Marketing at Covalent.

- Immutable: Once you create a contract, it is nearly impossible to change.

- Third Parties: They are not completely out-of-the-loop with Ethereum. For example, if you are creating a smart contract, you may need the help of an attorney to create the terms as well as to enforce them.

- Terms: The conditions in a smart contract can be ambiguous and complex. This can make it difficult to code on the Ethereum blockchain.

To deal with these problems, there has been work on Ethereum 2.0 (it is also referred to as Serenity). The goals are to increase the speed, scalability, and security of the blockchain.

For example, it will use the proof-of-stake (PoS) mechanism, which reduces the need for compute power to verify blocks. This is done where users provide cryptocurrency as collateral for the possibility of validating blocks. This is known as staking. For the most part, it's a way to gauge the commitment or "skin in the game."

The validators are randomly selected to mine the blocks. It's not about many computers competing to solve math problems. Rather, when a minimum number of validators verify the block – at 16,384 – it is then added to the blockchain. This should help improve the security of the network.

The blockchain will also have a different structure. It will use shards. Essentially, there will not be a single chain but chains that are created and managed in parallel.

With this new approach to verification and blockchain structure, Ethereum 2.0 will have more scale. The network capability will go from 30 transactions per second to up to 100,000.

But in the meantime, there are various other projects with the aim to improve Ethereum. Examples include Polygon, Arbitrum, Starkware, and ZK-Sync.

Then there have emerged alternative networks, like Solana, Near Protocol, Avalanche, and Ronin chains.

Solana

Solana is perhaps the biggest competitor for Ethereum. With it, you can create non-fungible tokens (NFTs) and decentralized applications (dApps).

Back in 2017, Anatoly Yakovenko and Raj Gokal created the Solana project. One of the biggest priorities was speed. Note that Solana can get to 65,000 transactions per second. The fee structure is also fairly low – especially when compared to Ethereum.

For the minting, Solana uses the PoS protocol. But it also has its own system called proof-of-history (PoH). With this, it's possible to verify if the transactions are in the right sequence. This is done by dividing the blockchain into different time periods and the validators are selected ahead of time (this is based on the PoS staking). For the most part, this allows for more agility and efficiency.

While this approach has seen good results, there are some nagging issues. With fewer validators, there is the concern that there is more centralization. For example, a large amount of the SOL tokens – which are the native ones for Solana – are owned by venture capitalists.

In early 2022, the price of the SOL was $116, and the total market value was $37.8 billion.[8]

Near Protocol

The Near Protocol may not necessarily be a catchy name. But this blockchain platform has been getting lots of traction.

In 2018, former Microsoft employee, Alexander Skidanov, and Ilya Polosukhin, launched the Near Protocol project. Over the years, the team has attracted some of the most renowned programmers in the world. For example, two have won the Programming World Championship twice.

For Skidanov, he is a fervent believer in decentralization and the power for the community. As a result, Near Protocol is focused essentially on the needs for developers. But there are features that make it user friendly. Consider that instead of using hash addresses, there are understandable written ones.

The Near Protocol system provides for smart contracts and dApps. It also operates with a PoS blockchain and uses sharding. This breaks up the network into manageable segments and the result is more scale.

As for the selection of validators, this is done by using an auction. The selections are for about every 12 hours or so.

Another key to the success of the Near Protocol is its powerful cloud infrastructure. It is based on serverless approaches and leverages a large number of systems across the globe.

For early 2022, the price of the NEAR token was $15.90, and the market capitalization was $10.5 billion.[9]

---

[8]https://coinmarketcap.com/currencies/solana/
[9]https://coinmarketcap.com/currencies/near-protocol/

Avalanche

On the Avalanche website, it says that its blockchain system is "blazingly fast, low-cost and eco-friendly." And this is not necessarily hype. For example, the transactional finality is under two seconds. By contrast, it is six minutes with Ethereum.

Avalanche is relatively new, with the launch in late 2020. The founders include two computer science professors, Emin Gün Sirer and Kevin Sekniqi, as well as Maofan "Ted" Yin, who is the creator of Facebook's digital currency project Libra (although, the social media giant would abandon it).

By far, DeFi is the main area where Avalanche has seen the most success. Then again, financial platforms need high speed and scale. Although, Avalanche has been investing more in the Metaverse, gaming, and virtual worlds.

As for the blockchain, Avalanche has a blend of different approaches – which it refers to as the Avalanche Consensus Protocol. This includes the classical protocols. These are extremely fast and environmentally friendly. Then there are the Nakamoto protocols. Yes, this is the traditional system that Satoshi Nakamoto developed for Bitcoin.

Avalanche's UI is similar to Ethereum's and runs on the EVM. You can also use existing Ethereum wall addresses. As for the dApps, they are compatible with the Solidity language.

In early 2022, the native token for Avalanche – which is AVAX – had a price of $84 and a market capitalization of $22.5.[10]

ConsenSys

Joseph Lubin has a diverse background. After graduating with a degree in Electrical Engineering and Computer Science from Princeton University, he worked at a lab for the development of autonomous music and robots. After this, he worked for a cryptographic payments business and then went on to create his own hedge fund. He would eventually become a VP of Technology in Private Wealth Management at Goldman Sachs.[11]

But there were key themes in his career – and they revolved around cryptography, engineering, and finance.

In 2014, he met up with Vitalik Buterin in Toronto. He was intrigued with his ideas and helped Buterin create Ethereum.

---

[10]https://coinmarketcap.com/currencies/avalanche/
[11]https://www.linkedin.com/in/joseph-lubin-48406489/

For Lubin, he saw a big opportunity to build a company, ConsenSys, on this emerging blockchain. The timing was definitely spot on. The result is that ConsenSys has become a go-to company for Ethereum.

The company has created the MetaMask wallet, which has grown to over 30 million Monthly Active Users (MUAs).[12] It has a strong presence in the USA, Philippines, Brazil, Germany, and Nigeria.

Next, ConsenSys has Infura. This is a leading development platform for Ethereum. There are about 430,000 developers on it and the on-chain ETH volume is over $1 trillion.

But ConsenSys has a myriad of other products, such as the following:

- Codefi: This includes nine tools to help businesses digitize assets.

- Diligence: This is a system for audits and security for smart contracts.

- Quorum: This is for testing networks.

ConsenSys has a long list of customers, which include some of the world's largest enterprises and governments. For example, the company helped the Asian Development Bank (ADB) create a DeFi system.[13] The focus is on connecting all the central banks and securities depositories among 13 countries in Asia and the Pacific region. The goal is to reduce the time to settle cross-border transactions from a few days to near real time.

In March 2022, ConsenSys raised $450 million in a Series D Financing at a valuation of more than $7 billion.[14] It came just after a few months from its other financing, which was for $200 million.

Lido

The move for Ethereum to staking will be important. However, there has been resistance from users to use this approach. Why so? Here are some reasons:

- Staking Has Lower Risks: While this can be reassuring, it does mean that the returns tend to be lower. Users often would rather use their tokens for more lucrative purposes.

---

[12] https://consensys.net/blog/press-release/consensys-raises-450m-series-d-funding/
[13] https://consensys.net/blog/news/adb-plans-to-make-cross-border-payments-more-efficient-with-blockchain/
[14] https://consensys.net/blog/press-release/consensys-raises-450m-series-d-funding/

- Locked Up: Staking means you cannot access your tokens. Again, this means tying up your assets, which weighs on returns.

- Expense: Currently, staking is not cheap. You need to put up a minimum of 32 ETH, which is over $90,000. Because of this, crypto exchanges have created systems to pool assets.

Then what to do? A startup, called Lido, has been building systems to help out. The company is a top provider of liquid staking services. As a testament to its success, the company has raised over $73 million.

Lido has more than 80% of the market, with more than $10 billion in staked assets.[15] There are about 76,000 crypto wallets.

With Lido, you can stake your assets without a minimum investment requirement. The company did this by creating a decentralized autonomous organization (DAO), which has allowed wider participation through more incentives. This has also helped to boost trust with the community. When Andreessen Horowitz invested in Lido, it purchased governance tokens for the DAO.

You can also use them for collateral for DeFi applications, which can mean generating better returns. This is done by the creation of a sophisticated derivative financial instrument. Lido currently is available for Solano, Terra, Kusama, and Polygon.

According to a blog from Andreessen Horowitz: "Lido democratizes staking. The Lido community's unwavering commitment to decentralization really stood out to us. They recognize that for their approach to succeed, they will need to create a fully trustless staking pool while also embracing alternative solutions."[16]

Private Blockchain

Blockchain's public ledger is a critical part of providing trust and security with the network. But this feature has its drawbacks. Simply put, there are certain organizations — such as highly regulated ones like banks and healthcare operations — that need very strong levels of privacy.

---

[15] https://techcrunch.com/2022/03/03/lido-raises-the-stakes-for-crypto-defi-investors-with-new-capital/
[16] https://a16z.com/2022/03/03/investing-in-lido/

This is where the private or permissioned blockchain comes in. There is a central authority that has certain requirements for entry.

Yes, the ledger is secure and to get access to it, a user needs to obtain permission from the central authority. The users can then operate the blockchain as they would if it were public. Think of this as partial decentralization.

Besides privacy, there are other advantages for private blockchains:

- Performance: Because of the smaller sizes of private blockchains, the speed is usually higher. This can be particularly important for enterprise applications that may need near real-time performance.

- Efficiency: The rules for becoming members of a private blockchain means that users are more focused on the use cases of the network. This will mean less congestion and fewer transactions.

The Linux Foundation has created a project to help develop private blockchains. It is called Hyperledger Fabric (note that there are other systems available like Corda, Ripple, and Quorum).

The system is highly customizable. You can mix other technologies within the private blockchain. You can also use it on-premises, the cloud, and hybrid environments. Then there are capabilities to integrate with legacy IT systems. In other words, the Hyperledger Fabric has been built for enterprises. Note that half the companies on the Forbes Blockchain 50 use the technology. These companies have revenues or valuations over $1 billion.[17]

An industry that has shown strong adoption for the Hyperledger Fabric is healthcare. Here are some use cases:[18]

- IBM Digital Health Pass: This is a private blockchain to manage and verify COVID-19 and other vaccination status. The system provides minimal personal data to the user.

---

[17] www.hyperledger.org/wp-content/uploads/2021/11/HL_Paper_HyperledgerOverview_102721.pdf
[18] www.hyperledger.org/blog/2022/03/29/hyperledger-powered-solutions-helping-to-reshape-healthcare

- Avaneer Network: This is a partnership of Aetna, Anthem, Cigna, Cleveland Clinic, HCSC, IBM, The PNC Financial Services Group, Inc., and Sentara Healthcare. They built a private blockchain to allow for better collaboration with healthcare services while having a lower need for administrative help. This system helps to manage 80 million patient lives and 14 million annual visits.

- KrypC Pharmaceutical Delivery Supply Chain Solution: This is a private blockchain that streamlines the communications between pharmaceutical companies and insurance carriers. The goal is to allow for the safe delivery of drugs and treatments. A key with the private blockchain is the use of a stringent audit trail.

Iron Fish

Elena Nadolinski has a strong background as a software engineer. She has developed applications for companies like Airbnb and Microsoft with C# and C++. For example, she developed the autocomplete search service for Airbnb.[19]

In early 2017, Nadolinski founded Iron Fish. At the time, she got very interested in crypto and thought there was an opportunity to develop technology for privacy. In all, she has raised about $33 million for her startup.

While there have been ways to provide for privacy with blockchain, they have usually been complex. The result is that this has created friction for consumer adoption.

For Nadolinski, she based her system on zero-knowledge proof (ZKP). Essentially, this is where a user – called the prover – can verify the information for another user – the verifier – without there being any more information disclosed. Interestingly enough, this protocol is not new. Back in the 1980s, MIT researchers Silvio Micali, Shafi Goldwasser, and Charles Rackoff created the theoretical basis for ZKP. The result is that you can make a transaction that has the privacy of using cash.

Regardless, achieving privacy is no easy feat. After all, blockchain is inherently transparent. This means there is the risk of tracing.

For Iron Fish, the mission is to be a complete privacy solution – not just for a particular blockchain.[20]

---

[19] www.linkedin.com/in/elenanadolinski/details/experience/
[20] https://a16z.com/2021/11/30/investing-in-iron-fish/

> ■ **Note**   Nadolinski came up with the name for her startup – Iron Fish – from reading about World War II. At the time, the US Najajo Code Talkers used this as the codename for a submarine.

Conclusion

At the heart of Web3 is the blockchain. In this chapter, we've taken a look at how this technology allows for decentralized peer-to-peer transactions. There is also a public ledger that provides a history of all the transactions, which cannot be changed. To create new blocks, the nodes on the network will mine them. This often means solving complex math problems.

The first real use case of blockchain was Bitcoin. This cryptocurrency has become dominant in the industry. But there have been the emergence of thousands other altcoins.

There has also been the development of an ecosystem to handle the cryptocurrency transactions. For example, there are exchanges as well as many wallets.

A major inflection point with blockchain – and Web3 – was Ethereum. This allowed for the creation of smart contracts. They have been revolutionary and have led to new businesses, such as NFTs and DeFi.

But Ethereum suffers from some problems, such as with high fees and difficulties with scaling. Because of all this, there are alternative platforms. Yet Ethereum remains that main one for Web3.

In the next chapter, we'll take a look at the Web3 tech stack.

The Web3 Tech Stack

The Platforms for a Startup

In the summer of 2017, Nikil Viswanathan and Joe Lau cofounded Alchemy. The business was actually in their San Francisco apartment.

Both Viswanathan and Lau were graduates in computer science from Stanford University. They had worked at companies like Google, Microsoft, Facebook, and Pinterest.[1] They also founded several companies.

But there was one that would be a rocket ship – Alchemy. From the start, the startup was focused on creating a development platform for the blockchain.

The growth accelerated at a fever clip in 2021. In April, the company raised $80 million in a Series B round at a valuation of $505 million.[2] Then by October, Alchemy did another fund raise. This time it was for $250 million at a $3.5 billion valuation.

---

[1] www.alchemy.com/company
[2] https://techcrunch.com/2022/02/08/alchemy-which-aims-to-be-the-de-facto-platform-for-developers-to-build-on-web3-raises-another-200m-and-is-now-valued-at-10-2b/

© Tom Taulli 2022
T. Taulli, How to Create a Web3 Startup,
https://doi.org/10.1007/978-1-4842-8683-8_3

But the company was not done. In February 2022, Alchemy raised $200 million at a $10.2 billion valuation.

Then again, the company was profitable and generating over $1 billion in value per month from its blockchain platform. Some of its marque customers included OpenSea, Dapper Labs, and Adobe. Alchemy's business model was to charge based on the usage of its compute resources.

The company was also very lean and did not use much of its capital. For example, there were fewer than 30 employees. No doubt, the company was selective with its recruiting – and this proved critical in creating a standout platform.

The case of Alchemy highlights the huge growth potential for Web3. But it also shows the importance of development tools. Because of the complexities of blockchain, there needs to be different approaches.

In this chapter, we'll take a look at what founders need to know about what's available and how to evaluate the tools.

The Web3 Tech Stack

The tech stack describes the tools for product development. These include libraries, platforms, IDEs, databases, web services, and so on.

There are certain types of tech stacks that have become quite common in the startup world. For example, there is MERN, which has the following systems:

- MongoDb: This is a NoSQL database.

- Express: This is a Node.js web framework. It helps with server-side activities like URL routing and HTTP requests and responses.

- React: This allows you to create dynamic front-end interfaces using JavaScript.

- Node: This is a JavaScript web server to run the applications.

With the MERN stack, you can create highly sophisticated web applications. Some of the companies that use this technology include UberEats, Instagram, and Walmart.[3]

---

[3] www.classicinformatics.com/blog/why-is-mern-stack-our-preferred-platform-for-startups-apps

Then what is the Web3 stack? Well, this is still evolving. It will probably take a few years until there will be standards like MERN.

But of course, founders cannot wait. They need to make decisions on the types of technologies to use. And yes, this means there are risks. First of all, there is the selection of the type of blockchain. Next, you will look at those tools that can best achieve your goals.

"Specific projects may require specific tools or programming languages, but I would encourage first principles learning around distributed systems architecture and encryption protocols, or for the front-end developer or designer, gaining competencies in how to express visually what is happening behind the scenes of a distributed network and how that brings value to the user," said Jennifer Hinkel, who is the Managing Director of The Data Economics Company. "Because these ways of thinking are, in some cases, a complete paradigm flip of architecture for 'Web2' platforms and applications, I think it's important for developers to spend time getting a firm grasp of the distributed architecture paradigm and its links to economic value."[4]

Hinkel also recommends that you ask these questions:

- Am I building an application?
- Am I building a platform?
- Am I building an infrastructure tool?

Of course, this will lead you to different tech stacks. "Depending on what you're aiming to build, you'll be relying on different levels of the technology stack, and therefore will have to make choices around what you build on and build with and what you need to be compatible with," said Hinkel. "If someone builds an infrastructure tool, it is true that they may also build prototype platforms and apps to prove out its use."

In Web3, the different components of the tech stack are divided into layers. We'll take a look at these next.

Layer 1

Layer 1 is the foundation of the underlying blockchain. It's what makes it operate, allowing for Bitcoin, Ethereum, and altcoins.

---

[4] From the author's interview with Jennifer Hinkel on April 4, 2022.

This is the low-level technology, which includes the complex network infrastructure, hardware, and connections. It makes it possible to facilitate the transactions and create and run smart contracts. For example, it's at Layer 1 where there are the consensus algorithms like proof-of-work (PoW), proof-of-stake (PoS), proof-of-reputable (PoR), and so on. This is also where the encryption is handled as well as the Ethereum Virtual Machine (EVM) is in operation.

For an infrastructure startup, a founder may need to work a Layer 1. This would also be the case if you are creating your own tokens or cryptocurrencies. But if you are building an application, then you really just need to have a basic understanding of this technology.

Layer 2

Layer 2 involves solutions that help improve the performance, and efficiency of the underlying Layer 1 protocols. Again, this is mostly for infrastructure startups.

As should be no surprise, the Layer 2 category has seen lots of growth. This is no different than what happened during the early days of Web1. The reason is that there needs to be the creation of a solid technology infrastructure to allow for consumer and enterprise applications.

For Layer 2, there are a variety of innovations that have helped improve the network, such as the following:

- PoS: This is much faster and environmentally friendlier than the original PoW protocol.

- Sharding: This has been critical in allowing more scale. There is no need to work on transactions on a sequential basis, but instead in different chunks or shards. Also, there is no requirement to have the nodes have a full copy of the blockchain.

- Block Size: This allows more transactions to be processed in each block. An example of a Layer 2 system for this is SegWit, which is for Bitcoin. By excluding the digital signature data, there has been more room per block.

Even with the enhancements, the user community may not be in agreement. Making changes can take time – and face resistance when it comes to the Layer 2 platforms. Because of this, there may ultimately be hard forks, which create new ones.

When it comes to Layer 2, there are certainly many options, and this is a challenge for entrepreneurs. It could mean that you may invest a substantial amount of resources on a platform that could ultimately be marginalized or even becomes obsolete.

The fact is that the core infrastructure will probably operate according the Power Law. This is a concept from statistics, in which a change in one quantity results in a larger change in another. For example, if you double the length of a side of a square, it will mean a quadrupling of the size.

What does this have to do with technology? It really is about the importance of standards. When one emerges, it generally dominates. This is what has happened with operating systems, whether Android, iOS, or Windows.

And the same is likely to happen with the core blockchain platforms. There simply will not be enough resources to keep building on multiple ones. Although, as of now, there has yet to emerge an Apple, Google, or Microsoft of the Web3 ecosystem.

To build scale, Layer 2 operators are providing financial incentives. This is often about paying third parties to create applications and solutions on their platforms. True, for entrepreneurs, this can mean quick money. But for the long run, it could be the wrong approach. For example, Microsoft did this with its mobile OS. But ultimately, it failed because Apple and Google became the dominant players in this category.

Keep in mind that Web1 provides a historical perspective. There was a huge amount of investment in the telecom infrastructure of the Internet. But this was overdone and there was an oversupply of resources. As a result, many of the players in the infrastructure space failed. This could very well be the case with the Layer 2 sector.

Something else to consider: from the Web1 phase, the big winners were not the infrastructure players. Instead, they came from the application side, such as Amazon.

Despite all this, there remains much to be done with Web3 infrastructure. Here's the viewpoint from an Andressen Horowitz blog: "On Layer 2 blockchains, scaling transactions and speed to meet growing demand has been a consistent challenge. The rapid growth in applications, which is the hallmark of this industry's success, will only exacerbate the need for dynamic and reliable infrastructure. In addition, programmability is one of the core benefits of blockchains, but smart contract languages may have unintended loopholes that hinder the interoperability and security of services and users' assets such as NFTs."[5]

---

[5] https://a16z.com/2021/12/06/investing-in-mysten-labs/

Layer 2 can certainly be confusing with Layer 1. But to get a better understanding, let's take a look at the so-called blockchain trilemma. This is about the tradeoffs between the following:

- Security: True, this is a problem with all technologies. But with blockchain systems, the risks of security can potentially be more severe. The reason is that there is often a reliance on using financial assets.

- Decentralization: This is about allowing peer-to-peer transactions with little friction.

- Scale: For there to be a truly global system for Web3, this is crucial. But with current blockchain systems, there are often problems with congestion and fees. The result is that the performance can be lacking – and this may mean lower adoption of Web3 technologies.

For Ethereum, it has done a good job with the first two factors. But as we've seen in this book, the third factor is often a problem. Perhaps the reason is the creators of Ethereum did not think this technology would be so popular.

OK then, so what does all this have to do with Layer 2? Well, it is generally about the applications on the Web3 platform. However, this really has been for creating technologies to help with the scaling – but without sacrificing security and decentralization. It has become a very big business, actually. And the growth is likely to continue for some time.

For the most part, Layer 2 is about finding ways to increase the speed of transactions – which is often called faster finality – and higher transaction throughput (which refers to transactions per second). Keep in mind that there are many startups gunning for this. There are also lots of top VCs that are investing substantial amounts.

In the next few sections of this chapter, we'll take a look at a few of the top startups in the Layer 1 and Layer 2 categories.

IoTeX

The Internet of things or IoT is a network of physical nodes, which use sensors and software. With this, it is possible to provide a connection to the Internet to allow for the exchange of information. Examples of IoT devices include home appliances, baby monitors, industrial tools, and even self-driving cars.

The IoT market is massive and is expected to grow at a rapid clip. According to McKinsey, the network will – by 2025 – have over 75 billion smart devices that produce 80 trillion gigabytes of data.[6] The value of this is estimated at $11 trillion.

Despite all this, there are nagging issues with IoT, such as with security, privacy, and integration. But Web3 and blockchain could help out.

This is the bet for IoTeX, which is a startup. The company, which was founded in 2017, is developing a decentralized Layer 2 IoT platform. It allows the users to have control over the data that their devices generate. They can even monetize this, which is done with its MachineFi technology. Note that there is the IOTX token.

IoTeX also creates their own devices. For example, there is Ucam, which is a sophisticated home security camera. Then there is the Pebble Tracker. This is a smart GPS system, which collects temperature, humidity, and air quality data – in real time.

IoTex uses an EVM-compatible blockchain, which allows for dApps and smart contracts. The platform has been operating since early 2019 and has had a high degree of stability.[7]

Mina Ecosystem

Launched in 2017, Mina Ecosystem is very light. The blockchain size is only 22 kilobytes or about the size of a few tweets. Because of this, it has proven to be quite useful for smartphones and other devices.

The Layer 2 Mina Protocol was also built with strong security and privacy functions. To this end, it uses zero-knowledge proof applications and smart contracts. This means that the system verifies data without the users having to give up their data. Mina Ecosystem has used this technology to create its own flavor of smart contracts, which are called zkApps. Another advantage is that it is easy to program the applications.[8]

In March 2022, Mina Ecosystem raised $92 million.[9] This was certainly a major validation of the zero-knowledge smart contract category.

---

[6] https://onboard.iotex.io/why-iotex-matters
[7] https://onboard.iotex.io/introduction
[8] www.zdnet.com/finance/blockchain/mina-ecosystem-gets-92m-financing-led-by-ftx-three-arrows-capital/
[9] https://cryptoslate.com/mina-ecosystem-raises-92m-to-build-the-lightweight-blockchain-for-web3/

According to Brian Lee, a partner at FTX Ventures: "Mina's lightweight blockchain architecture allows the protocol to reach a new level of decentralization by enabling everyone to easily participate in the network. That, combined with its native data-privacy capabilities makes it a unique LI with massive potential to shape the future of Web3."[10]

Mysten Labs

In 2021, Evan Cheng, Sam Blackshear, Adeniyi Abiodun, and George Danezis cofounded Mysten Labs. Before this, the team worked at Novi, which was the crypto division at Meta. The cofounders helped to create the Move programming language as well as the Diem blockchain.

While Meta had the benefit of lots of resources, it was difficult to make progress. One of the main reasons was the onerous regulatory scrutiny.

So, for the cofounders, it seemed that a better path was to create a startup. For Mysten Labs, the focus is on building advanced infrastructure technology for the Layer I blockchain called Sui. This is a next-generation version of Diem, which uses a PoS protocol that is permissionless. You can also use the Move language to create smart contracts.

The big differentiation then? It has potentially unlimited throughput or transactions per second.[11]

As for the business model, it is similar to the approach for many infrastructure operators. That is, the company generates revenues by getting a percentage of the tokens from the different blockchains. It is essentially an ownership model.[12]

StarkWare

Uri Kolodny is a serial entrepreneur. He cofounded OmniGuide, which developed precise optical laser scalpels for minimally invasive surgery. He then went on to start TimnaTimna. The company created an ultrasound therapeutic product for cardiovascular problems.[13]

---

[10] www.prweb.com/releases/92m_capital_raise_led_by_ftx_ventures_and_three_arrows_capital_puts_the_mina_ecosystem_in_position_to_become_leading_hub_for_zero_knowledge_smart_contracts/prweb18561853.htm
[11] www.theblockcrypto.com/linked/138813/web3-infrastructure-startup-mysten-labs-unveils-its-layer-1-blockchain
[12] www.cnbc.com/2021/12/06/mysten-labs-raises-36-million-from-andreessen-horowitz-crypto-fund.html
[13] www.linkedin.com/in/urikolodny/details/experience/

But after this, he would move into the software business. For example, he launched Mondria Technologies, which focused on a new type of declarative programming language for visualizing data.

The experience would prove critical for his Web3 play – Starkware. Founded in 2017, the company is a top developer of Ethereum scaling solutions. The two main ones include StarkEx and StarkNet. They make it easier for people to create dApps on the Ethereum network.

StarkWare has created its own language, which is called Cairo. It has been in production since June 2020. Although, you do not have to use this language for StarkWare. The company has been building transpilers for other systems.

StarkWare uses a zero-knowledge rollup. This means that the verification is based on combining transactions, which speeds up the performance and allows for lower fees. StarkWare has also invested heavily in its security infrastructure. As for the customers, they include many top Web3 providers like Immutable, dYdX, and ConsenSys.[14]

Since inception, StarkWare has raised $173 million.[15] Some of the investors include Sequoia Capital and Paradigm.

Matter Labs

When Alex Gluchowski launched his Web3 startup – Matter Labs – in late 2018, he did not have a crypto background. The two prior companies he started included a camper rental marketplace and a website for holistic lifestyles. Yet he gained valuable skills from these ventures.[16] He learned how to build modern and scalable web platforms, manage remote teams, implement payment and bookkeeping systems, create compliance automations, and work in international markets.

Regarding Matter Labs, it is based on the Layer 2 protocol called zkSync. For more efficiency, the funds for a smart contract are on the mainchain, but the computation and storage are handled off-chain. This essentially means that the transactions are rolled up to a block. In fact, Ethereum co-founder Vitalik Buterin wrote in his blog that for the medium to long term, the zero knowledge rollups "will win out in all use cases…"[17]

---

[14] https://techcrunch.com/2021/11/16/sequoia-backs-blockchain-scaling-startup-starkware-at-2-billion-valuation/
[15] www.crunchbase.com/organization/starkware-industries-ltd
[16] www.linkedin.com/in/gluchowski/?originalSubdomain=ae
[17] https://vitalik.ca/general/2021/01/05/rollup.html

Matter Labs has built an intuitive user experience, but has also been strong with security features. This has helped to gain traction with customers, especially in the DeFi space.

The Matter Labs platform uses Zinc, which is a framework for creating smart contracts. This is important since zero-knowledge-protocol frameworks generally lack these capabilities. The syntax of Zinc is similar to the Rust language. Although, Matter Labs is working on a Solidity implementation.

In late 2021, the company raised $50 million. Andreessen Horowitiz, which invested in the round, wrote a blog about the Matter Labs: "The activity on Ethereum L1, between DeFi, governance, NFT trading, DAO creation, and gaming has surpassed our wildest imagination in terms of creativity and progress. One way to explain the ingenuity we're seeing comes back to the core idea of self-sovereignty inherent to cryptography, and essential to the ethos of web3. zkSync is building (and enthusiastically hiring!) for the next generation of developers and will unleash rippling waves of originality into the already vibrant Ethereum ecosystem."[18]

Optimism

Jinglan Wang is a rarity in the Layer 2 infrastructure world. She is one of the few female CEOs and cofounders of a top startup in the industry: Optimism.

Since college, she has been fascinated with blockchain. She would become the co-president of the MIT Bitcoin Club, where she greatly expanded her network of industry contacts.

She did not finish her degree and instead started a company called Eximchain. Then she went to Zcash and Nasdaq, where she was a product manager for blockchain projects.

She would actually get a scar because of Ethereum. How so? When ETH hit $300, she was at a bar with friends. She was so excited that she fell out of her chair and split her ankle open.[19]

But it was Optimism that would become her breakout venture. In March 2022, she raised $150 million in a Series B round from Andreessen Horowitz and Paradigm. The valuation was $1.65 billion.[20]

---

[18] https://a16z.com/2021/11/08/investing-in-matter-labs/
[19] https://newsletter.thedefiant.io/p/the-defi-scaling-engine-is-here-and-141?s=r
[20] https://techcrunch.com/2022/03/17/paradigm-and-a16z-back-ethereum-scaling-startup-optimism-at-1-65b-valuation/

The core technology of Optimism is different from a zero-knowledge rollup. Instead, it uses an "optimistic rollup." This is about using a group of validators to verify transactions, not cryptography. At the time of the funding, the Optimism platform had over $500 million in locked value.[21]

One of the keys to the success of Optimism has been mostly to stick to the Ethereum approaches.[22] This has leveraged the large ecosystem, but has made it easier to get started.

Note   There is often confusion between Layer 2 and sidechains. But they are very different. A Layer 2 system is built on the Ethereum platform. A sidechain, on the other hand, runs parallel to it. It is a separate blockchain, with its own security and consensus approaches. A top sidechain is Polygon.

Offchain Labs

Ed Felton is 59 years old. Yet his age has not been a problem with being the co-founder and chief scientist of a red-hot Web3 startup, Offchain Labs. Actually, Felton has a deep academic background. He graduated from the California Institute of Technology in 1985 with a degree in physics and got his Ph.D. at the University of Washington. He wrote his thesis about communication protocols for parallel processors.

In 1993, he joined the faculty at the Princeton University in the Department of Computer Science. He would then serve as the Chief of Technologies for the Federal Trade Commission as well as the Deputy US Chief Technology Officer for President Obama.[23]

The origins for Offchain Labs started with Felton's research efforts at Princeton. He met his cofounders there – Steven Goldfeder and Harry Kalodner – and they started to create a Layer 2 platform called Arbitrum. This started in 2015. The goal was to make Ethereum available to anyone.[24]

Offchain's platform is based on the optimism rollup, and it has gained lots of traction. In 2021, there were more than 350 teams using it. Some of the partners include companies like Uniswap and Chainlink.

---

[21] https://techcrunch.com/2022/03/17/paradigm-and-a16z-back-ethereum-scaling-startup-optimism-at-1-65b-valuation/

[22] https://a16z.com/2021/02/24/investing-in-optimism/

[23] www.linkedin.com/in/ed-felten-275171/

[24] www.prnewswire.com/news-releases/offchain-labs-rolls-out-arbitrum-one-ethereum-scaling-solution-to-the-public-and-announces-120m-in-funding-301365642.html

The company raised its Series B for $100 million and the lead investor was Lightspeed Venture partners. The valuation was set at $1.2 billion.[25]

In a blog post, Lightspeed investor Amy Wu had this to say: "A lot has been written about how L2s work and the differences between optimistic and zero-knowledge roll-ups, and which are theoretically better. In deciding to lead Offchain Labs' Series B, we focused on the most important thing: what is easier and better to use for developers."[26]

Layer 3

Layer 3 is known as the application layer. This is where you have programs like dApps as well as the protocols that power them. These apps can be virtually anything. However, much of the development has been with areas like NFTs, gaming, and DeFi.

There are two main parts of Layer 3. First, there is the application itself, which is what the user interacts with. This often involves scripts and APIs.

Next, there is the execution. This is about managing the rules and conditions of the smart contracts on the blockchain. Essentially, this is the underlying code. Thus, there is coordination of actions between the application and execution.

In chapters 7 and 8, we will look deeper at the Layer 3 programs and systems. And as for the rest of this chapter, we will cover the different types of Web3 frameworks and libraries as well as the languages.

Web3 Frameworks and Libraries

It's common for people to treat the words "library" and "framework" as if they were the same. But there are important differences.

Granted, both are code bases, and they provide often-used features, such as for authentication, UI, or security. And many of them are based on JavaScript or TypeScript. Libraries and frameworks can definitely be a big help in speeding up development projects.

---

[25] https://techcrunch.com/2021/08/31/offchain-labs-raises-120-million-to-hide-ethereums-shortcomings-with-arbitrum-scaling-product/
[26] https://medium.com/lightspeed-venture-partners/offchain-labs-how-arbitrum-is-transforming-ethereum-scalability-510685b0a159

So, what are the differences then? It comes down to the concept of inversion control. Basically, with a library, you have more control over the workflow of the program. A framework, on the other hand, provides its own paths. This is similar to the use of an API.

For Web3, there are a myriad of libraries and frameworks. Let's take a look:

- Web3.js (Library): This provides a set of functions for on-chain transactions and components for Ethereum nodes. This basically makes it easier to handle the JSON RPC mechanism for the transmission of the data (this is a standard format). This is done by using JavaScript code. Web3.js also works seamlessly with Node.js web applications and Electron desktop programs. It's common for developers to use the Metamask browser extension with this library, which is an in-browser Ethereum wallet.

- Ethers.js (Library): This uses JavaScript and TypeScript to provide four main modules to interact with Ethereum. Ethers.provider allows for the transactions; ethers. conrtract helps to deploy and manage smart contracts; ethers.utils provides the formatting and processing of data for dApps; and ethers.wallet makes connections to Ethereum addresses.

- oo7.js (Library): Yes, this is named after James Bond. In terms of the technical aspects of this library, it's about using reactive expressions or bonds. This essentially makes it possible to understand when values are triggered on a smart contract for Ethereum.

- Truffle: Consensys created this in 2017. Truffle is a comprehensive framework that has easy-to-use tools for creating, debugging, and deploying smart contracts for Ethereum. It also has integrations with popular Web frameworks like React, Angular, and Vue. With Truffle, you can use Solidity or JavaScript for the coding. Another helpful feature is that this framework manages the network artifacts. Truffle also includes Ganache, which is a rich set of GUI components.

- Hardhat (Framework): This allows you to create a marketplace – with little work. This handles all the complex matters of managing digital assets. The framework supports Django and Ruby on Rails web frameworks. Hardhat also has strong debugging capabilities for Solidity, which are bolstered by a rich ecosystem of plugins.

- OpenZeppelin SDK (Framework): Launched in 2018, this is a framework built on the Python language and provides components for NFTs and other tokens. A major advantage is that it has strong security features built in. The OpenZeppelin SDK comes with its own development environment, which is called Jesta. But perhaps the most powerful function of this framework is the ability to upgrade existing smart contracts.

- Brownie Framework (Framework): This is based on Python and provides for creating smart contracts on Ethereum. For the development, you can use Solidity or Vyper. The Brownie Framework uses the web3.py library, which has shown to work on intensive environments.

Note   An oracle allows for hybrid smart contracts. These work with both on-chain and off-chain data. A top solution in this category is Chainlink. It is built on a variety of technologies like Java, C++, Python, and Node.js.

Web3 Languages

As we've seen, Web3 relies on a variety of languages. Some have been around for many years like Java, JavaScript, C++, and Python. But there are some languages that were built specifically for blockchain. Some of the top ones include Solidity and Vyper.

Regardless, there are common tools for Web3 development. There will usually be the use of Node.js and a code editor. The editor can be just a plain text application for command line coding. Or, you can use a sophisticated IDE (a popular one is the Remix IDE). Then there will typically be the use of Web3 frameworks and libraries. And finally, a developer will work with a wallet to access the nodes.

At a very high level, there are often two types of developers. There is the backend developer, who has expertise on the intricacies of working with the blockchain. Next, there is the front-end developer. This person will focus on the UI, workflows, and design. And there usually does not require to be a significant understanding of the underlying technologies.

Note that there remain challenges with Web3 development. Here's a look:

- Immature: The development tools are still in the nascent stages. The result is that the UI's can be cumbersome. There is often the lack of core features in the development environments.

- Costs: Gas fees and other charges can be a major hindrance. For the most part, coders may be hesitant deploying apps. If anything, this means that the activity will be mostly with experimenting, such as with testnets.

- Fragmentation: There are already many development tools on the market. This makes it difficult for coders to find the best one. There is also the risk that there will be much investment in a tool that ultimately fades in popularity.

- Immutability: When a smart contract is added to the Ethereum blockchain, you generally cannot change it. This is certainly difficult, since the code is often far from perfect. Although, there are some workarounds, such as working with proxies to point to another smart contact.

But such problems are to be expected. They happened with other new platforms, such as with iOS or Android.

The good news is that there is much investment in building out the tools. There will also be more of a focus on low-code and no-code offerings, which will help to democratize Web3 development.

Now let's take a look at some of the languages.

Rust

Rust has a similar syntax to C++. But it makes it easier to deal with memory leaks and other issues. There is also a high level of performance. This is especially the case when processing enormous amounts of data.

Note that the 2021 Stack Overvlow Developer Survey, which involved more than 80,000 developers, named Rust the most "loved" language.[27] This was the same ranking for the six consecutive prior years. Just some of the companies that use the language include Amazon, Meta, Google, and Microsoft.

But Web3 is becoming a catalyst for growth for Rust. For example, platforms like Polkadot and Solana use the language to allow for the creation of smart contracts.

It's true that there is a significant learning curve. But if you want to write high-performance Web3 applications that have strong security, Rust is a pretty good option.

---

[27] https://insights.stackoverflow.com/survey/2021

▨ **Note**   In late 2021, Jack Dorsey tweeted: "rust is a perfect programming language."[28]

Solidity

In 2014, Gavin Wood started the development of the Solidity language. The goal was to make it easier to create dApps for the Ethereum blockchain. At the time, the development was done using C++. While it was extremely powerful, it was also complicated.

By 2015, Wood finished the first version of Solidity. He also had the help of other top developers like Christian Reitwiessner, Alex Beregszaszi, Liana Husikyan, and Yoichi Hirai.

Now Solidity shares important features from C++. Note that both languages are object-oriented. This means you can organize an application into different components, which allow for reusability, and the inheritance of code and logic for other parts of a program. Object-oriented approaches tend to allow for more efficiency and scale. It can also be easier with collaborating with other coders.

Solidity remains quite popular with development on Ethereum. But you can use the language for many other blockchain platforms like Tron, Hedera Hashgraph, Avalanche, and Binance Smart Chain.

In terms of the syntax, it is similar to JavaScript. This has made it easier for programmers to learn the language.

The most common IDE (Integrated Development Environment) for Solidity is Remix. This is built to allow for the writing, running, debugging, and deploying of smart contracts on the blockchain. Keep in mind that the necessary libraries are included in the distribution. There is also a seamless integration of the Ethereum Virtual Machine (EVM).

Vyper

Vyper is for developing smart contracts for the Ethereum Virtual Machine and is No. 2 in the category, behind Solidity. The creator of this language is Vitalik Buterin (the original name was Viper). Then other contributors took over the project.

---

[28] https://twitter.com/jack/status/1474263588651126788?ref_src=twsrc%5Etf
w%7Ctwcamp%5Etweetembed%7Ctwterm%5E1474445866681475077%7Ctwgr%5E%7Ctwco
n%5Es3_&ref_url=https%3A%2F%2Fwww.thecoinrepublic.com%2F2021%
2F12%2F26%2Frust-is-jack-dorseys-favourite-programming-language%2F

One of the hallmarks of Vyper is its security features. Compared to Solidity, they are more seamlessly part of the development process. It is also easier to implement the compiler.

Then there is audibility. This means that a non-technical person can look at the Vyper code and have a general idea of the workflow.

The syntax is similar to Python's. Vyper has some object-oriented features like inheritance.

However, because of these benefits, there are fewer features compared to Solidity. The language is also less free from.

Note   To help improve the security of Solidity, there is the annual Underhanded Solidity Contest. The goal is to write "seemingly innocent and straightforward-looking Solidity code which actually contains malicious behaviors or backdoors."[29] For 2022, the contest is to build a DeFi platform, and the first prize is a ticket to Devcon VII Bogota.

QuickNode

QuikNode is a blockchain infrastructure platform. Some of its marque customers include PayPal, Adobe, OpenSea, and Fireblocks. The company has over $40 million in venture backing.

With QuickNode, developers can quickly setup and integrate a blockchain system. A key to the success is the speed. You can access Ethereum, Bitcoin, Polygon, and other nodes within milliseconds or less. Another key to the success for the company has been the agility of its development team. In 2021, it added support for a new blockchain every month or so.

Growth has been particularly strong. During the first quarter of 2021, QuickNode was serving more than two billion requests per day for a community of close to 20,000 developers.[30] To scale this, the company has built a multi-cloud infrastructure with more than 15 regions across four continents.

But the growth is likely to continue for some time. A study from Markets and Markets research predicts that blockchain infrastructure will increase at a compound annual rate of 67% – reaching $40 billion by 2025.[31]

---

[29] https://underhanded.soliditylang.org/
[30] www.prnewswire.com/news-releases/leading-blockchain-infra-provider-quicknode-raises-35m-series-a-led-by-tiger-global-301409773.html
[31] www.prnewswire.com/news-releases/leading-blockchain-infra-provider-quicknode-raises-35m-series-a-led-by-tiger-global-301409773.html

QuickNode operates from an easy-to-use panel. With this, you get the following:

- Rich Analytics: You can get metrics on the performance of dApps, such as what smart contract methods are being called the most and when.

- Monitoring: You get details on the trends in the traffic that streams into your nodes on an hourly, daily, weekly, or monthly basis.

- Debugging: There are helpful tools to detect and fix problems with your dApps.

- NFT Fetch Tool: No longer will you have to scrape logs. QuickNode has an API that aggregates a wallet's NFTs.

- Archive: The system tracks all states for smart contracts and logs them for future use.

- Trace: You can re-execute a transaction with different types of data.

- Integrations: There are many, such as for Metamask, Augur, and MyCrypto.

Developer Views

So what are some of the approaches and views of Web3 developers? Well, here's a look at this from a company called GeodeFinance, which is a developer of staking technology.

First, here are the takeaways from 0xCypher:[32]

- Ethereum: "Currently, in our application, records of dozens of data sets belonging to each wallet should be kept in Ethereum. That's because keeping them in a central database completely forces our users to trust us. That's why every web component that appears on our interfaces comes from Ethereum, a decentralized database. So no one, including me, can change the numbers at will. Any updates are made to the extent that smart contracts allow, which is why I recommend every defi and web3 user make sure that contracts are written securely and without errors."

---

[32] From my interviews with 0xCypher and Pacific.

- Tools: "We first find an RPC (remote procedure call) endpoint. If a node is running on your local machine, a port of your computer is connected to Ethereum. Every call you send to a URL such as 127.0.0.1/8000 can now withdraw or send your balance and contract information from Ethereum. After connecting the provider, you also need to encode all the contract interactions. We are lucky that web3 libraries can be used in both Javascript and Python quite effectively."

- Proof-of-stake: "The proof of stake-based version 2 of the Ethereum named the 'beacon chain' is deposit-based. The main way I use Web3 libraries is to send API calls to these chains and load the data I get into our own smart contract via oracle services. Normally you can do this by simply calling a function in both Python and Javascript. But we use a multi-signature system called Gnosis to ensure data security with a secure consensus, which means we encode and sign the input data and send it to web3."

Here are the views from Pacific:

- Web3 Experience: "The main question and the hardship about all of these marvelous benefits of Web3 is the responsibility that comes with it. 5 billion people have access to the internet and still, most of them are not even comfortable with using it. Also, using Web3 is not as comfortable as using the usual Web2. Web3 is being built upon smart contract blockchains such as Ethereum, Avalanche, Solana, etc. To operate freely on these blockchains, you need to have all the responsibilities for your wallet, you need to interact with lots of different types of Decentralized applications and mostly and at the very basic level you need to know what you are doing within and on these decentralized applications. All of these factors can look frustrating at first for most people and it is frustrating when we consider the majority to be honest. There needs to be a whole paradigm shift, for Web3 to be the new standard, and in my point of view, it will take some time."

- Developing on Ethereum: "Ethereum has been around for nearly ten years. It has been the first one around with the smart contracts that gave the idea of money that is programmable. Also, Ethereum has a strong foundation with a highly capable team and the community. This strong foundation makes Ethereum attractive. From a developer perspective, there are much more resources on the internet for Ethereum than any other blockchain. You can find answers with several search engine queries. This is not the case for most of the blockchains even that are EVM compatible. Technology accumulates around Ethereum, which results in bigger communities, higher developer support, and thus higher adaptability. Tied with that attractiveness, the number of Decentralized apps that are being built around Ethereum is higher than other blockchains combined. This gap is slowly closing, however, the Ethereum dominance on Web3 infrastructure will be there for a while."

- Startups: "The main problems with Web3 are that it still can be considered as it is in its infancy and there is an adaptability problem. So for me, an interesting start-up should be solving these issues about Web3 and Ethereum. OpenSea and the NFT ecosystem have done a great job of arousing the interest of non-technical people and getting them into the space. With that showcase, we have seen that anybody can interact with the blockchains with a little effort. Even though the idea of OpenSea is still similar to the Web2 companies, there needs to be a transitional form, from centralized to decentralized for most people to understand what is really going on with the Web3."

- Hyper-Financialization: "Everything that users do in Web3 is through their wallet, unlike the current Web2 paradigm where people think that they are using most of these platforms for free. Of course, this is not the case but it is perceived that way. From what we know from behavioral economics, most of the people are loss-averse. The absolute value of -$10 dollars is much more than the absolute value of +$10 in people's eyes. So in terms of Web3 adaptation for the general public, an interesting start-up should build up an architecture where people won't feel like they are losing money when they act on a blockchain or Web3 platform."

- Alternatives to Ethereum: "For me, Avalanche is a great alternative to Ethereum, especially if you're a new user or a small-level investor who's only got a little bit of extra cash to experiment and learn with. Avalanche offers EVM compatibility with its C-Chain, and lower transaction costs with higher throughput thanks to the probabilistic nature of its consensus protocol. Also, Avalanche blockchain can have some advantages on scalability with its Subnets. In a future where Web3 is the new standard, leap-forward technologies like Subnets can still ensure decentralization while removing the burdens of scalability issues."

Conclusion

In this chapter, we got an overview of the Web3 tech stack. It is still evolving, and this can make development challenging for entrepreneurs. Picking the wrong platforms and tools can blunt a startup's progress. But this is always a risk for any nascent industry.

But despite all this, there is an emerging structure to the tech stock. The foundation is Layer 1, which involves the core technologies for the blockchain. Next, there is Layer 2. This is about systems to help improve the performance and efficiency. During the past few years, there has been significant interest from VCs in Layer 2.

And finally, there is Layer 3. This is about the applications, such as for DeFi, NFTs, gaming, and so on.

In this chapter, we also looked at the libraries and frameworks for Web3, such as Web3.js, Truffle, and Ethers.js. We also got an overview of the languages like Solidity, Vyper, and Rust.

As for the next chapter, we will look at building the Web3 team for a startup.

The Web3 Team

The Roles Needed for Startup Success

With the strong growth in Web3 from 2020 to 2022, there have been many high-profile tech executives that have moved from megatech companies to startups in the space. Here are some notable examples:

- Brian Roberts: He had been the CFO of Lyft since 2014. But in late 2021, he took the CFO spot at OpenSea.[1]

- David Marcus led Novi, which was the crypto unit for Meta.[2] He had an extensive background in the fintech space, having also been the president of PayPal as well as on the board of Coinbase. So then what will he do next? It looks like he has plans to create his own Web3 startup.

---

[1] https://techcrunch.com/2021/12/06/long-time-lyft-cfo-departs-to-become-cfo-at-nft-marketplace-opensea/
[2] https://techcrunch.com/2021/11/30/facebooks-top-crypto-executive-david-marcus-is-leaving-the-company/#:~:text=Facebook's%20top%20crypto%20exec-utive%20David%20Marcus%20is%20leaving%20the%20company,-Lucas%20Matney%40lucasmtny&text=Facebook%20parent%20company%20Meta%20is,the%20company%20later%20this%20year

© Tom Taulli 2022
T. Taulli, *How to Create a Web3 Startup*,
https://doi.org/10.1007/978-1-4842-8683-8_4

- Surojit Chatterjee was a vice president of Google, where he relaunched Google Shopping. But he saw more opportunity in the startup world and joined Coinbase as the company's chief product officer.[3] It certainly was the right move. Within 14 months, his stock options were worth more than $600 million.[4]

The megatech companies have been trying to deal with this. Part of strategy has been to increase the compensation packages. But given the high valuations in the Web3 industry, this may not be enough. The megatech companies may need to instead have to move aggressively with crypto and blockchain. And yes, this should help drive even more progress and validation.

But despite all this, recruiting is not easy for startup founders. There are thousands of companies looking for talent. This means that recruiting is often one of the most time-consuming duties for a founder.

So in this chapter, we'll take a look at some of the key roles for the Web3 team of a new venture.

■ **Note**   Founders have been using creative ways to recruit. For example, it is common to put "We're hiring" in the subject lines of Twitter bios and LinkedIn profiles. The same message is often at the top of a startup's website.

The Competition for Talent

A key advantage for recruiting Web3 talent is the excitement of the industry. For many potential candidates, they were not a part of the Web1 or even Web2. Web3 is a chance to be a part of a transformative event in tech history.

Next, there is much work to be done. There will need to be new innovations. And not just for software and systems. There will also need to be a rethinking of business models and go-to-market strategies.

Finally, there is the allure of making substantial amounts of money. Granted, there are still plenty of people who are idealistic and want to change the world. But there are probably many more that are driven by the potential for striking it rich.

---

[3] www.reuters.com/article/us-coinbase-moves/google-shopping-product-executive-leaves-for-cryptocurrency-exchange-coinbase-idUSKBN1ZS2MS
[4] www.nytimes.com/2021/12/20/technology/silicon-valley-cryptocurrency-start-ups.html

Yet there are some issues to keep in mind. The reality is that there are not many experienced blockchain and crypto developers. A study by Electric Capital estimates the number at only about 18,000.[5] For those working in Web3, it's under 5,000. By comparison, there are over 16 million developers that use JavaScript.

Given the demand in the Web3 industry, there will certainly be much more growth in the number of qualified developers. But it will take time to increase the numbers. The underlying concepts of Web3 can be difficult. There will even need to be some un-learning of traditional development concepts.

Given all this, there should be no surprise that compensation packages for Web3 and crypto talent have skyrocketed. For example, at Coinbase, a senior protocol engineer makes an average of $362,000 a year and the pay for an infrastructure engineer is $672,550.[6] This is at roughly the 75th percentile of the pay ranges for similar tech companies.

Thus, for an entrepreneur, you need to have a compelling message to recruit Web3 talent. Consider that it's common for startups to include this in their job ads – usually at the top. Here are some examples:

- "At Matter Labs, we are building zkSync: a blockchain scaling solution secured purely by cutting-edge cryptography. Our mission is to scale Ethereum to billions of users, fully preserving its most valuable properties — permissionlessness, trustlessness, and resilience, — in order to protect and enhance global economic freedom."[7]

- "Mysten Labs believes that decentralized and open protocols are the bedrock of the internet of value. This is why at Mysten, we are creating foundational infrastructure to accelerate the adoption of decentralized protocols based on blockchain technologies."[8]

- "Valora Inc's mission is to unlock access to financial opportunity so everyone can create and share value without barriers. We believe every person should have access to the information, education, and tools needed to build wealth. When everyone has the potential to prosper, our world will be a more supportive and interconnected place."[9]

---

[5] www.ft.com/content/16eaf1b9-08fb-4454-a4eb-ac662cdd8590
[6] www.fastcompany.com/90739257/leaving-faang-web3-jobs
[7] https://boards.eu.greenhouse.io/matterlabs/jobs/4011492101
[8] https://jobs.lever.co/mystenlabs/6430fa4e-5f8e-4f06-9764-dead784b0907
[9] https://boards.greenhouse.io/valorainc/jobs/4379733004

- "[Alchemy's] mission is to bring blockchain to a billion people. The Alchemy Platform is a world class developer platform designed to make building on the blockchain easy. We've built leading infrastructure in the space, powering over $105 billion in transactions for tens of millions of users in 99% of countries worldwide."[10]

However, having the right message is just a minimum. You will likely need to raise venture capital or get the support of an incubator or accelerator program. If you cannot pay competitive salaries, you will have a tough time putting together the right team.

In fact, when it comes to job ads for Web3 companies, you might want to mention the general funding history. This will help build more confidence in the company.

OK then, so now let's take a look at the various roles for a Web3 team.

Developer Advocate

For Web3 infrastructure and tools categories, there is often the use of open-source software. This allows for leveraging innovation, but also for providing wider distribution of the technology.

But for a project to be successful, there needs to be a strong and vibrant community. This is where the Developer Advocate comes in. This person will cultivate the relationships with the developer community. This is done with a variety channels:

- Social media and collaboration platforms like Twitter, YouTube, Telegram, Discord, and Reddit.
- Virtual and in-person workshops.
- Hackathons.
- Conferences.

The Developer Advocate will have a rare blend of technical and soft skills. This person should understand a computer language like Rust, Solidity, or C++. There should also be experience using platforms for creating smart contracts.

---

[10] https://jobs.lever.co/alchemy/70c9f8e9-85dc-464e-9426-2b0a6c56669b

In terms of the soft skills, the Developer Advocate should be a strong communicator. They can do such things as

- Be a speaker at an event.
- Write blogs.
- Create podcasts.
- Put together engaging videos, such as for tutorials or demos.
- Craft social media posts.

Even though a Developer Advocate will likely have a technical background, they will not spend any of their time coding. There will simply not be enough time. Rather, the duties will often include interacting with the company's developers as well as the engineering teams.

Community Manager

Whether a startup is focused on infrastructure or applications, there is usually a need to build a strong community. In the early stages, you want to make sure you can connect with early adopters. They will generally be more engaged with your software. They will also provide useful feedback and tell other users about your company.

This is why it is common to hire a community manager. No doubt, this person will help with content on social media channels and blogs. But there will be other critical duties, including:

- Develop a strategy for targeting the right groups.
- Come up with a social media and blog calendar.
- Manage a newsletter.
- Help with customer issues, comments, and questions. There will certainly need to be collaboration with customer support and product teams.
- Provide assistance with online and live events.

While a community manager does not have to be a programmer, they should have a high-level understanding of blockchain and crypto. A startup may also want to provide some training.

The main qualifications for a community manager include good communication skills – and yes, passion for the product and industry. This person will also need thick skin. Communities can sometimes get unruly and harsh. A good community manager will know how to keep their cool.

Creativity is also important. For example, a community manager can help come up with engaging memes. These can certainly be a good way to attract and retain users. Or a community manager can help create promos, contests, and giveaways.

Something else: A key role for the community manager is education. Let's face it, users do not want to be "sold" to. They want to get value. What's more, when it comes to new users, they will have lots of questions about Web3.

General Counsel

For entrepreneurs, it can be tempting to not focus much on legal and compliance. This is often just red tape that can hinder growth, right? To some extent, this is true. There are definitely examples where avoiding the legal niceties has paid off. Just look at cases like Uber and Airbnb. They were largely able to thrive because their services were in legal gray areas.

But Web3 is different. Because it usually deals with tokens – which have monetary values – there are legal landmines. For example, a government agency could shut down a startup.

This is why there needs to be a good legal foundation – and this should begin in the early phases of a startup. If anything, some of the highly successful startups in crypto took this approach.

This is not to imply you need to hire a full-time lawyer. This is probably too much for a startup. Rather, a more common approach is to have a lawyer on retainer.

This person can help with the following:

- Provide the right legal structure for the startup, such as with an LLC, C-Corp, or cooperative. There will then likely be the creation of a DAO (Decentralized Autonomous Organization).

- Help with regulatory matters. They are evolving. They are also different from country to country. But a lawyer will help navigate all this.

- Assist with the creation of tokens. This can be a complex process, which involves setting up a foundation. This is usually offshore.

- Help with onboarding users. This means that there will be the right legal consents to protect the startup.

Ideally, you want a lawyer who has firsthand experience with the issues of Web3. But unfortunately, there are not many that have this background. What to do? Well, you can look at a lawyer's skillsets that are similar to what is needed with Web3. Here are some examples:

- Experience with structuring legal entities and funding them. This is perhaps the most important for a startup.

- Background working in the financial services industry or fintech. This would include having dealt with regulations, such as with anti-money laundering statutes or the Bank Secrecy Act.

- Experience with privacy laws like the General Data Protection Regulation (GDPR), California Consumer Privacy Act (CCPA), and Health Insurance Portability and Accountability Act (HIPAA).

- Knowledge of federal and state securities laws.

- Understanding of laws regulating product disclosures.

You also want an attorney that is licensed by a state bar. You can also do a background check at lawyers.com and by contacting the local bar association.

Finance or Accounting Manager

A finance or accounting manager is crucial for a startup. Because of the new business models, there needs to be a system to manage the transactions.

This person does not have to be a full-time employee. Instead, you could bring on a contractor or hire an accounting firm.

Here are some of the typical activities for a finance or accounting manager:

- Build and manage the month-end close process.

- Record the monthly journal entries, transactions, and reconciliations.

- Check for any reporting discrepancies.

- Help with tax compliance.

- Prepare financial reports, such as the balance sheet, income statement, and cash flow statement.

- Assist with preparing budgets.

- Oversee vendor setups and accounts payable.
- Prepare forecasts for the company and the various departments.

For these functions, you may want a couple people. The reason is to avoid conflicts of interest. After all, if there is only one person involved, there may be a temptation to embezzle funds.

You should focus on those candidates that are Certified Public Accountants (CPAs). They have gone through extensive education on all the core aspects of accounting. They also will have audit experience.

It's true that a CPA may not have an extensive background with blockchain and Web3. But then again, they should be able to learn about the key topics. The CPA will also help with other non-Web3 aspects, such as invoicing, working with ERP (Enterprise Resource Planning) programs, general accounting, and so on.

Front-end Developer

A front-end developer focuses on the UI of a website or mobile app. In terms of skillsets, they usually are a blend of design and scripting. For example, a front-end developer will need to know HTML, CSS, and JavaScript.

It's critical that this person have a good sense of the user experience. This is especially important in Web3 since the concepts can be complicated or new. This means that the front-end developer will spend lots of time about where to place messages and buttons. There may also be the use of animations. What's more, the UI must work on multiple form factors, whether a tablet, smartphone, or desktop screen.

Here's how a job ad from Alchemy describes the role of a front-end developer: "You will help delight blockchain developers with sleek interfaces and intuitive visualizations that make their lives easier. Your work will be the first thing users see and will define the blockchain development experience for developers and enterprises globally."[11]

Here's a look at other tasks for a front-end developer:

- Help with the wireframes and visual design.
- Provide feedback during code reviews.

---

[11] https://jobs.lever.co/alchemy/b1c6aa94-0055-4de3-83fb-5b2a0ad97d20

- Come up with best practices for the front-end design.

- Debug the code.

- Collaborate with software engineers, project managers, and designers.

- Look at ways to provide security and scale for the design.

- Help with A/B testing.

Having a background in blockchain is definitely helpful. But a front-end developer does not need to be an expert in this technology or even know languages like Solidity. Rather, this person will have a background in various front-end libraries and frameworks like React, GraphQL, Angular, Bootstrap, and VueJS. It is also helpful to have some experience with database and cloud platforms like AWS. Finally, it is great if the developer has a background in putting in production apps that have large user bases.

Backend Developer

The backend developer focuses on the server-side of an application. This often means using or writing APIs. These will often integrate with the front-end of the application. Because of this, there is usually much coordination between front-end and backend developers.

The backend developer will certainly need a solid background with programming. Often this will mean having a computer science degree. Although, a candidate may show that they have taken various online courses and have received certifications for them. In terms of the languages to understand, the common ones include C, Java, Python, Golang, C++, Rust, and .Net.

Backend developers will usually need a good understanding of how to work on hosted cloud services, such as from Amazon, Microsoft, or Google. Then there will be a need to know about databases. This could be a traditional relational database, such as from Oracle, or a NonSQL version. In fact, a backend developer can be helpful in providing feedback on what types of databases make more sense for the startup's use cases.

A good backend developer will provide clear documentation. This is absolutely critical. Let's face it, there will usually be a group of backend developers. So, they all need to be in sync. But there will be ongoing hirings and you want to make sure that these developers can get up to speed as fast as possible.

Let's take a look at some of the other duties and activities for backend developers:

- Work with version control and DevOps to help streamline the process. This means knowing developer tools like Jenkins, GitLab, or GitHub.

- Develop best practices for the backend application process. Often this is about focusing on goals like reliability, low latency, and high throughput. There should also be ongoing efforts to find improvements with these metrics.

- Put together unit tests for the software. They can be a combination of manual and automated testing.

- Develop custom tools to help build a more robust infrastructure.

Blockchain or Smart Contract Engineer

Early in the startup, you will likely need engineers who understand blockchain and smart contracts. Often this means there must be experience with Ethereum and the Solidity language.

The engineer will create the protocols for the smart contracts and help provide for a solid architecture. There will also need to be a focus on providing security as well as optimization of the performance. As noted in Chapter 3, platforms like Ethereum have problems with scale. An engineer can help deal with this, such as by evaluating and selecting third-part systems.

Here are some of the other duties for this person:

- There will need to be strong hands-on experience with writing, deploying, and testing smart contracts.

- Come up with best practices for the protocols for the upgrades and versioning for the networks. This is essential since there is so much dynamic change in the Web3 world.

- The engineer will help with the UI and explain what is required to make for a good smart contract.

- Develop audit protocols. This is essentially about making sure the smart contracts are stable.

- Collaborate with various departments, like R&D, data science, product management, recruiting, and the executive suite.

- Keep track of analytics to detect problems and find opportunities for improvement.

Security Engineer

In building the Web3 application or platform, you need to have a well-thought-out security infrastructure. Trust is vitally important. If there is a breach, then the startup could easily fizzle out.

Consider a job ad from Web3 startup Dapper Labs. The title was a "Senior API Engineer – Security Hardening, Bots, Scalability" and here was some of the description: "We are open to awesome engineers across a variety of specialties but in particular would love to talk to engineers with consumer API hardening and protection experience. The Top Shot and Dapper APIs are constantly being bombarded by increasingly sophisticated bots and fraudsters. The ideal candidates for this role have worked on high-value targets before – e-commerce gateways, web poker, crypto – and know what to expect."[12]

Here are some of the activities for a security engineer:

- Perform static analysis (SAST). This is automated analysis of source code without executing the application.

- Perform dynamic application security testing (DAST). This is about looking for security vulnerabilities by simulating attacks while an application is running.

- Develop best practices for security.

- Look for vulnerabilities with third-party dependencies.

- Conduct research on the latest security developments.

- Harden applications by using industry standards like CIS benchmarks.

- Use automation tools and configuration management systems.

In terms of the experience of a Web3 security engineer, the candidate should have a background with applied cryptography and blockchain. But there should also be a good understanding of security for web authentication and protecting data. Finally, there should be knowledge about distributed systems and microservices.

---

[12] www.dapperlabs.com/join/position?id=1fff7d65-6645-4bcc-b7ab-960ecdd9aad8

Recruiting

For a startup, there probably will not be an in-house recruiter. Instead, this may be outsourced to an agency. This can still be expensive, though.

As a result, a company will still need to do its own recruiting as well. And often this is for the founders and executives. This will demonstrate to the candidates the importance of getting the best talent. For example, for the executive leadership team, the myriad of speaking engagements, conferences, and meetups can be great opportunities to find strong candidates.

Although, a startup might want to hire a recruiting assistant or HR person. They can handle the administrative details, such as tracking the candidates, documenting the interviews, and doing the screening. They can also help with the sourcing. This could mean using resources like LinkedIn.

It's also never too early to think about a company's culture, which is very important for recruiting. Here's how Coinbase looks at its own: "There are a few things we look for across all hires we make at Coinbase, regardless of role or team. First, we look for candidates who will thrive in a culture like ours, where we default to trust, embrace feedback, and disrupt ourselves. Second, we expect all employees to commit to our mission-focused approach to our work. Finally, we seek people who are excited to learn about and live crypto, because those are the folks who enjoy the intense moments in our sprint and recharge work culture."[13]

There's a saying in the tech world that "the next five hires are the most important when starting a company." This is certainly spot on. The reason is that this is where the culture will be formed. During this stage, you need to have a good sense of the vision of the company. If not, this could make it difficult to have a unified team that scales.

Given the dynamic changes with Web3, it can be difficult to get a sense of what the goals should be. There is always a temptation to evolve with the changes.

But ultimately, you want to take a long-term approach. What will be needed for the next ten years?

Again, Coinbase is a good example of this. The founder and CEO, Brian Armstrong, started the company in 2012. He became part of the YCombinator program and raised $150,000. At the time, he split with his partner because they disagreed about the vision of the company.

---

[13] www.coinbase.com/careers/positions/4054455

Armstrong was a firm believer in blockchain and bitcoin. However, he realized that it was too complicated for many people. So he wanted to create a marketplace that made it easier for anyone to buy and sell Bitcoin. He also aimed to create a system that focused on compliance. Armstrong thought this would be key to building trust.

Interestingly enough, there were many people who thought his idea was terrible.

But Armstrong persisted and he convinced many employees, investors, and customers about his vision.

Fast-forward to today. Armstrong is one of the wealthiest persons in the world, with a net worth of over $6 billion. As for Coinbase, it is a clear leader in the crypto world.

According to Roger Lee, a venture capitalist in Battery Ventures and an early investor in Coinbase: "The key lesson is to think long-term. Coinbase could have taken a bunch of short-cuts in building out their solution—for example, ignoring and minimizing compliance, regulations and so on. But they chose the long game and are accruing huge value as a result."[14]

Recruiting Best Practices

Recruiting is certainly challenging. A person's resume might look standout. But the person could still turn out to be the wrong match for the venture. Often this is when there is a clash with the company culture.

Even a few bad hires can be problematic. It could slow the growth of a company. It can also encourage other top employees to leave.

So how can you be a better recruiter? Well, there are some best practices. But it's also important to keep in mind that success is often about practice.

Before you recruit, though, there are some preliminaries. First of all, you need to put together clear-cut requirements for what you are looking for. True, this may seem basic. But then again, it's common for the requirements to be vague and this can mean attracting and selecting the wrong candidates. Make sure to spend time on what you are looking for.

Next, you should look at ways to improve the message and vision for the company. You want to make the opportunity as exciting as possible.

---

[14]www.forbes.com/sites/tomtaulli/2021/04/14/coinbase-ipo-an-early-investors-takeaways/?sh=63ad32a9f653

You also need to come up with goals and metrics to track the performance of the hiring process. This will not be very exact, especially in the early stages. But you still need to come up with some benchmarks – and you can change these over time.

With Web3 recruiting, you will probably have difficulties in finding people with relevant experience. The reason is that many of the technologies are fairly new. If you have a job ad that says you are looking for a Solidity programmer that has ten years' experience, you will probably be laughed at.

"Recruiting is one of the toughest parts of any tech startup," said Denis Mars, who is the CEO and founder of Proxy. "But it's even tougher for new categories. So, what I look for are those candidates who want to solve hard problems. And yes, there are many problems to be solved with Web3."[15]

He points out the example of Google, which has hired tens of thousands of talented engineers. "The company was solving a tough problem – that is, searching effectively all the information on the Internet," he said. "It was very interesting to computer science PhDs."

Mars looks for candidates that have completed their own independent projects. One example was a developer who used Bluetooth technology that allowed for peer-to-peer communication. In other words, it was able to do this without the need for Internet access.

Another popular way to gauge the skills of a developer is to setup a code challenge. Although, make sure to have a reasonable deadline and focus on a certain element of Web3.

In some cases, a startup will use pair programming. This is a code challenge, but two developers will work on it. You want to get a sense of the collaboration and communications skills.

With the limited supply of tech talent, you have little choice but to look outside the United States. Because of this, many Web3 companies are remote-first organizations or fully remote.

Although, this does not mean there should be no contact. For example, you can set up events to bring people together. There can also be periodic meetings where all the company's team members meet up.

Then what about sourcing talent? As mentioned earlier, LinkedIn is a good option. It definitely helps that you get a resume and listing of projects.

---

[15] From my interview with Denis Mars on April 12, 2022.

But there are other effective channels to find Web3 tech talent, such as:

- Job Boards: General purpose platforms like Indeed and ZipRecruiter can be useful. But there are also job boards specific for crypto and blockchain. Examples include Angel, CryptoJobs, and Crypto Jobs List.

- Talent Marketplaces: These are generally focused on freelancers and contractors. One of the top platforms is UpWork. Such a service can be a good option for a startup because you can get a sense of the person's capabilities. Ultimately, they could become employees.

- Social Media: Spend time reading Twitter, Reddit, and other channels that focus on Web3.

- Referrals: Ask your own developers if they have friends who would be good candidates. Often these may be the best prospects.

You should spend time creating a compelling career page. It should not just be a listing of the jobs either. Instead, provide the vision for the company and the values. You should also have photos and videos of the team.

Compensation

The high compensation levels in the tech industry are certainly a major barrier. But startups do have some advantages. In fact, with a Web3 company, there may be the opportunity to provide crypto tokens as part of the salary. Such digital coins can ultimately be worth significant amounts of money. However, there can be complex tax issues. We'll cover this topic in the last chapter of this book.

Next, equity is another way to attract top-notch talent. Some of the early crypto companies like Coinbase have minted many millionaires.

With options, you can provide a strong incentive for employees to stay on board. This is done by using vesting. This means an employee must remain as a part of the company for a certain period of time to get the equity or stock option.

A common approach is to have vesting for four to five years. For example, suppose you hire a hotshot developer and grant a stock option for 20,000 shares. If the vesting is for four years, the employee will earn 5,000 shares each year.

But suppose that an employee leaves after two years. In this case, they can exercise – or purchase – 10,000 shares. But they will forfeit the remaining 10,000 shares of the option.

Now, in some cases, the option grant may backfire. This happens when there is a huge surge in the valuation of the company. Thus, an employee may do minimal work in order to keep vesting the options. This is often referred to as VIP or vesting in peace.

Yet it can be extremely difficult to avoid this problem. The good news is that – for many high-performance people – they will strive to do great work.

For the types of equity compensation, there are two main categories. One is the employee stock option. This gives you the right to buy a fixed number of shares at a fixed price for a period of time.

Let's take an example. Suppose you hire someone and grant an option for 5,000 shares. At the time, the stock price of your startup is $2 a share. This will also be the exercise price for the option or what the employee will pay for the shares.

Suppose that your startup does extremely well, and the stock price goes to $20 a share after two years. The employee has vested 2,000 shares. They can purchase all of these for a total of $4,000 or $2 multiplied by 2,000. In other words, the employee will have a gain of $16,000.

The next type of equity offering is the restricted stock grant. This means that you issue the shares to the employee but there is vesting.

Let's continue with our prior example. Instead of granting an option for 2,000 shares, you make a restricted grant for the same number of shares. But to get the value of these, the employee will have a two-year vesting schedule. Using our example, in two years, your startup will transfer ownership of the 2,000 shares to the employee.

But there is a potential problem. The taxes could be at the ordinary rate, not the favorable capital gains rate (which has a maximum of 20%). But there is a way to deal with this: the 83b-1 election.

This is how it works. When you get the restricted stock grant, you will pay for the shares. In our example, you will write a check for $2,000. Then you will send a simple document to the IRS within 30 days. Also, if you miss this deadline, there is no recourse.

OK then, so how much equity should you allocate? There is no clear-cut answer for this. But the first step is to set up an option pool. This is a percentage of the company's equity that is for the granting of options or restricted stock. This can range from 5% to 25% of the outstanding shares.

In the early days of a startup, the equity allocations can be significant. For example, the first few nonfounding employees may get 1% of the outstanding shares. Then the next ten or twenty may receive 0.50% and so on.

However, there are certain employees where you will grant ever larger allocations – regardless of the stage of the startup. Note that it is not uncommon for a CEO to get 5% to 10% of the outstanding shares.

Finally, when it comes to putting together an option plan, you should seek the assistance of a qualified attorney. This is something that you want to make sure that is done correctly. You do not want to be in a position where your company falls out of compliance or you have to pay an unexpected tax bill.

■ **Note**   According to ZipRecruiter, the average salary for a blockchain engineer is $154,550 or $74 per hour. As for a Solidity developer, it is $127,5000, and it's $94,674 for a smart contracts developer.[16]

Reskilling

Since many of your developers may not have deep experience with Web3 or blockchain, you will have to look at ways to educate your team. There are different bootcamps that can be a big help. There are also online education platforms like Coursera, PluralSight, and Udemy that have useful and affordable courses.

But there are still many gaps. Because of this, your startup may have to put together some of its own courses. True, this will take time. But the long-term impact is likely to be very positive. Besides, you can focus on those areas that have the most impact for the success of your venture.

You can also set up programs to allow your experienced developers to be mentors. This can be rewarding for everyone. It can also allow for faster learning.

Conclusion

In this chapter, we looked at the key team members for a typical Web3 startup. They include community managers, legal experts, front-end developers, backend developers, financial managers, and so on.

---

[16]https://revelo.io/blog/hire-web3-developers

Finding this talent is no easy feat and the compensation is not cheap. And this is likely to last for many years. But there are ways to help with recruiting. You can leverage equity compensation and perhaps the use of tokens. You should also have a compelling vision that attracts top talent.

The reality is that recruiting is a must-have priority for startups. It's also something that should be hands-on with the founders and executives.

Even when you hire developers, you will probably need to provide training. While there are good education programs, you might need to come up with your own courses.

Being a remote organization is probably the right option too. Finding talent often means looking overseas.

As for the next chapter, we will take a look at DAOs or Decentralized Autonomous Organizations, which provide the governance for Web3 platforms.

Decentralized Autonomous Organizations (DAOs)

Governance for Web3

In November 2021, Sotheby's auctioned a first edition copy of the US Constitution (there are only 13 in existence). As usual, there were various wealthy bidders who participated. But interestingly enough, there was a Web3 entity that entered the fray.

It was called ConstitutionDAO. As the name implied, it used a Decentralized Autonomous Organization (DAO) for its entity. This allowed it to raise money to make a bid from many people for the US Constitution.

© Tom Taulli 2022
T. Taulli, *How to Create a Web3 Startup*,
https://doi.org/10.1007/978-1-4842-8683-8_5

The ConstitutionDAO raised over $40 million from 17,437 persons.[1] To do this, it created its own token, which was called $PEOPLE. This was based on the Ethereum platform by using a smart contract. Juicebox handled the transaction processing. In terms of the marketing, ConstitutionDAO primarily used Twitter and Discord. But of course, there was considerable PR that helped to gin up interest.

Those who made contributions would not become owners of the US Constitution. Instead, they would have governance rights. For example, they could vote on matters like where the document should be displayed.

ConstitutionDAO was unique since it was for the purchase of a physical item, which is fairly rare in the crypto world. This actually added to the complexities of the DAO structure.

But in the end, ConstitutionDAO did not prevail. Hedge fund billionaire, Kenneth Griffin, made the winning bid. He agreed to pay $43.2 million for the document.[2] But he believed in the main goal of ConstitutionDAO – that is, to make the US Constitution available to the public for free. All the contributors of the DAO received refunds and the entity was closed down.

This episode definitely showed the importance of this governance structure. It has become the primary one for Web3. So yes, entrepreneurs need a good understanding of DAOs – and we'll do this in the chapter.

The Origins of DAOs

Traditional corporate structures have central authorities. Consider the C-Corporation. To manage the organization, there is the CEO who makes the day-to-day decisions. There is also the help of other executive officers, such as the CFO (Chief Financial Officer), CMO (Chief Marketing Officer), the General Counsel, the Chief Human Resources Officer, and so on.

Then there is the board of directors. This is a small group – say five to ten people – who provide help with the strategic direction of the company. They also have the power to pay a dividend, approve executive compensation, and vote on mergers and acquisitions.

As you can see, the traditional corporate structure is highly centralized. True, the shareholders do have the power to vote on limited matters, but they are generally passive.

---

[1] www.wsj.com/articles/copy-of-constitution-sells-for-43-2-million-as-crypto-group-is-outbid-11637285144
[2] www.wsj.com/articles/citadel-ceo-ken-griffin-outbid-a-group-of-crypto-investors-for-copy-of-u-s-constitution-11637352087

As for a DAO, it's about being a decentralized governance structure. All the members of the community have more power and participation. In fact, there are no CEOs or other executive officers. There are also no boards of directors.

Note that the DAO structure is in the nascent stages. The first one was called The DAO, which was launched in April 2016.[3] From the start, it got lots of traction and raised over $150 million. The goal was to provide funding for interesting blockchain and crypto projects.

But unfortunately, the success would quickly turn into a nightmare. Hackers were able to breach the systems and take substantial amounts of crypto. The DAO was actually warned, but this was ignored. Ultimately, the problem was a coding error.

But the problems would only continue. There was an adverse ruling from the Securities and Exchange Commission. The DAO would eventually need to be shutdown.

Despite this, the DAO structure has been able to evolve and improve. There are many examples of large entities that have done quite well.

But it's important to keep in mind that there continue to be many complexities and unresolved matters. If anything, it is similar to the early days of C-Corporations and LLCs. There had to be the evolution of case law to refine these structures.

Because of this, when it comes to setting up a DAO, you do need the help of an attorney. Granted, it's not easy to find one with much experience in the category. But the good news is that there are important parallels between traditional structures and DAOs.

How Does a DAO Work?

A DAO needs a goal or a purpose. But it can be anything. However, there are some general guidelines for setting up a DAO.

First of all, you will need to create the rules. As much as possible, try to be specific and find areas where there could be problems. This is where an attorney can be helpful.

With the rules, you will embed them into the smart contracts. They will essentially automate many of the actions of the DAO. You will then need to audit and validate them.

---

[3] www.linkedin.com/pulse/launch-failure-first-dao-waceo/?trk=organization-update-content_share-article

Next, you will need to fund it. Often this means creating a token (there is actually a built-in treasury for this). As a result, there is an incentive to keep up the DAO.

But this is not completely automated. A DAO usually needs people to provide some level of management, say with the treasury. For this, service providers will usually get paid in tokens.

You can issue more tokens to reward the stakeholders. The tokens can also be used as a way for the community to make purchases, such as for NFTs or virtual land on the Metaverse.

Then there is the launch of the DAO. This is when it becomes part of the blockchain. At this point, the changes are only allowed with the voting of those who have the tokens. This is done by putting together proposals. There is also transparency. After all, the proposals and voting history are recorded on the blockchain.

But what if the rules of the DAO are violated? In this case, it will be locked.

■ **Note** Billionaire investor Mark Cuban tweeted this about DAOs: "The future of corporations could be very different as DAOs take on legacy businesses. It's the ultimate combination of capitalism and progressivism. Entrepreneurs that enable DAOs can make $. If the community excels at governance, everyone shares in the upside. Trustless can pay."[4]

There are various types of DAOs available. Here's a look:

- Protocol DAOs: This is a project that is focused on leveraging Ethereum for DeFi applications. Some of examples include Aaave, Compound, and MakerDAO.

- Social DAOs: The word "social" can mean many things. But for a DAO, it is a broad way of describing a platform that has a strong community element. That is, it's about a place where people share a common interest. Some of the DAOs in this category are Seed Club, Friends with Benefits, and FiatLuxDAO.

- Collector DAOs: These are generally for NFTs that represent albums, artwork, and videos. Some of the Collector DAOs include Flamingo DAO and PleasrDAO.

---

[4]https://twitter.com/mcuban/status/1399498071873134592?lang=en

- Creator DAOs: These are targeted at super fans, such as for a music group. Usually, the DAO will issue an NFT. This can provide benefits like VIP passes, discounts on merchandise, and early access to events.

The Benefits of DAOs

We have already looked at some of the advantages of DAOs. For example, they can be quite effective in pooling the resources of a community. This can mean purchasing high-priced items.

Next, a DAO provides for transparency. All the transactions are on the public blockchain. This helps to bolster the trust for the platform as well as guidance for the community.

And yes, there are the potential financial rewards. In some cases, people have made millions from a DAO.

But there is something else to consider. A DAO helps to mitigate the principal–agent problem. In this case, the principal is the main owner or stakeholder of an entity, and the agent is the person or persons that make the decisions.

With a traditional structure like a corporation, there can be glaring conflicts. For example, a CEO may focus on short-term efforts to bolster their compensation. How many times have there been cases where they have departed with million-dollar packages – but have left the company in worst shape?

In some cases, an agent may engage in high-risk activities. If this person does not have a large stake in the entity, then this approach could have an attractive risk-reward profile. However, this puts the principal in jeopardy.

But with a DAO, there is better alignment. The participants serve both roles as principal and agents. There is also the strict enforcement of the rules that are embedded in the smart contracts.

DAOs Versus the Law

A key advantage of a traditional corporation is limited liability. This means that the shareholders generally are not on the hook for a company's liabilities. For example, suppose you own 1,000 shares of ABC Corp. – for which you paid $20,000 – and the company loses a lawsuit for $10 million. However, the company only has $1 million in the bank and its assets are $500,000. In this case, the plaintiffs cannot sue you personally to collect on this judgment. You are only liable to the extent of your equity. So if the stock price goes to zero, the most you can lose is the initial $20,000 investment.

Limited liability is critical because it makes it more attractive for people to invest in companies. In fact, this legal concept has been one of the biggest factors for the popularity of the corporate structure.

Now, as for DAOs, there is generally no recognized limited liability. This could ultimately reduce the opportunities for expanding the uses of this structure.

Yet lawyers have found creative ways to deal with this. For example, they will set up legal "wrappers" to provide protections. This essentially means embedding the DAO inside a corporate structure like a C-Corp or LLC. However, there should be caution. A change in regulation could make the strategy unworkable.

There's a temptation for entrepreneurs to just set up a DAO and not create a legal entity. But this can often be a bad approach. Keep in mind that there will actually be a default legal structure – that is, a general partnership. This is when two or more people join together for some type of business purpose. Each state has its own laws and regulations for general partnerships. There is also unlimited liability for the partners. Interestingly enough, you will often have this relationship with partners that are anonymous.

It's true that there is no need to register a general partnership with the state. However, the legal consequences can be significant and could hamper the progress of the DAO.

There is another important distinction between a DAO and a traditional corporation. The law treats the traditional corporation as a "person." This may sound strange. But it is another powerful concept. It means that a traditional corporation can sign contracts, hire people, own intellectual property, be sued, and so on. As for a DAO, it currently does not have this legal status. And this can be another limiting factor.

But in the years ahead, there is likely to be changes to the law, which will provide more protections and guarantees with DAOs. Note that Tennessee and Wyoming have already passed legislation for this.[5] Both states allow for registration of DAOs and have specified various rights.

In the case of Tennessee, it looks like the goal is to make the state the go-to place for crypto and Web3. There is already a thriving tech community in Nashville. But with new laws for DAOs, this should help increase the growth.

---

[5] www.nashvillescene.com/news/pithinthewind/tennessee-becomes-second-state-to-pass-dao-legislation/article_ecbd4cbe-b5e2-11ec-abe0-77a2385be512.html

According to State House Rep. Jason Powell (D-Nashville), the legislation will make "Tennessee the Delaware of DAOs. With this new business structure, Tennessee will be a beacon for blockchain investment, new jobs and investment. Just as Delaware became a hub for traditional LLCs or South Dakota for credit card companies."[6]

Countries are also pursuing similar strategies. In early 2022, the Republic of the Marshall Islands (RMI) allowed DAOs to register as a legal entity.[7] The first entity to use this was Shipyard Software's Admiralty LLC.

The Caymans and Switzerland have become popular nations to set up DAOs. Although, these countries do not have a specific law for registration.

But DAOs are still in the formative stages. It will be far from clear how things will progress. "At present, I think a DAO is mostly an ethos about how an organization will be run—more decentralized, more democratic—and an approach to bake these concepts into operations and governance," said Jennifer Hinkel, who is the Managing Director of The Data Economics Company. "How to exactly operationalize a DAO, including how to set one up in a legal framework and fund it, are thornier questions and the topic of debate among many startup attorneys."

The Problems

For some of the most fervent advocates in Web3, the belief is that DAOs will ultimately become the dominant form of business organization. Some think that the next mega tech company will be a DAO.

This very well may turn out to be true. But there are still many problems with DAOs.

Let's take a look:

- Unintended Consequences: A DAO is only as good as the rules that it is based on. But unfortunately, it is extremely difficult to anticipate problems. What if there is a mistake in the code? A change in the law? Or a natural disaster? The algorithm may not be programmed for these "outlier" events – and this could lead to a malfunction of the DAO. One approach is to use

---

[6] www.nashvillescene.com/news/pithinthewind/tennessee-becomes-second-state-to-pass-dao-legislation/article_ecbd4cbe-b5e2-11ec-abe0-77a2385be512.html
[7] www.globenewswire.com/news-release/2022/02/15/2385589/0/en/The-Republic-of-the-Marshall-Islands-Formally-Recognizes-DAO-Incorporation.html

sophisticated technologies like AI. But again, even this is far from perfect. AI is based on having access to large amounts of data and putting together the right algorithms. For a DAO, there just may not be enough for good outcomes.

- Decentralization: While using legal wrappers is a good strategy, it does mean that there will likely be less decentralization. After all, there will still be the traditional governance approaches like executives and a board of directors.

- Authority: For a DAO, the smart contract may handle some of the core decisions. But what about the other decisions? Well, these are generally for the creators. Note that this process may not be transparent. There may also be conflicts of interests, especially when it comes to issuing new tokens. Who will they go to? Back to the creators?

- Complexity: It's common to use entities across different countries. While this can provide protection, there is also more complexity and expense. Creating offshore entities can take months to establish.

- Regulations: In early 2022, the Biden Administration issued an executive order about crypto and blockchain. It was mainly a way to encourage research on the issues. But this will likely be the basis for regulations on crypto and Web3. The result is that it could make it unpredictable for structures like DAOs.

- Participation: Ironically, it is generally low for DAOs. But this should not be surprising either. Let's face it, voting in political elections is often tepid. The same goes for corporate proxies. As for DAOs, the lack of participation is likely due to several factors. First of all, people may not have the time to vote. Next, the issues might not really matter to them. For example, if there is a vote on a technical matter or for the operations of the DAO, it probably will not get much interest.

But perhaps the biggest disadvantage of a DAO is that it could lead to bad strategic decisions. If Apple Computer or Microsoft were run as this type of entity, would it have had the same success? It seems unlikely. The impact of Steve Jobs and Bill Gates were incalculable. But of course, their decisions were often far from transparent (especially with Jobs) and there was significant centralization.

"Many organizations that are currently attempting to create DAOs are adopting a 'progressive decentralization' approach, because for projects to be successful, they do need to start with a handful of highly motivated leaders or a core team," said Hinkel. "Immediately jumping into having an organization guided by a group of potentially thousands of people, whether through a tokenization of voting rights or other mechanisms, is expensive and cumbersome, and has slowed down some DAO projects."

An exception is for those projects that have substantial scale. They have been able to prove the value of the DAO and can raise enough capital to make it run properly.

"While these projects get an outsized amount of attention, they are the exception, not the rule," said Hinkel. "When you draw back the curtain on many of the most successful DAO projects, they have significant backing from traditional VC and investor sources as well as community support, which requires all of the same entrepreneur and fundraising skill sets in terms of networking, and building investable business fundamentals as a Web2 company would have."

Rather, it might be better for entrepreneurs – in the early stages – to have a hybrid approach. On the one hand, there will be traditional corporate and contract mechanisms. Then, in terms of the community for the Web3 project, there could be a focus on the DAO.

Here are some other best practices to consider:

- Security: Unfortunately, this remains a problem with DAOs. There continue to be breaches – and some of them have resulted in the theft of substantial amounts of money. In other words, when it comes to creating DAOs, security should be priority No. 1.

- SubDAO: This is a smaller segment within a larger DAO. The idea is to breakdown the decision-making into different categories. This can help to improve the participation and effectiveness of DAOs.

- Limits: It's usually a good idea to have a small number of decisions for the DAO. Otherwise, the users may get overwhelmed, and they will just avoid voting.

- Incentives: You can provide more tokens to members, so as to help increase the engagement of the DAO.

- Delegation: A common problem with DAOs is getting a quorum for proposals. A way to deal with this is to allow members to delegate their votes.

- Domain-based Voting: This means that for those users with more experience on certain matter, they should have more voting power. "An example is that you would rather have the votes of professional marketers to be weighted higher in a marketing campaign decision than say a software engineer," said Nik Kalyani, who is the founder of Decentology.[8]

Nick Casares, who is the head of product at PolyientX (a Web3 tools developer for NFTs), has some other best practices to consider. He is an expert on DAOs. For example, he is a contributing member for the ATX DAO.

Here are some of his suggestions:

- Establish a north star: "DAOs are an innovative vehicle to share resources and collaborate on a mission with people worldwide. To take full advantage of a DAO's potential, participants must define a clear mission and purpose. There is no right or wrong mission, but DAO members must agree on a north star to guide the DAO toward its goals."

- Lead without hierarchy: "The lack of hierarchy within a DAO provides a unique challenge that often leads to a sense of lacking leadership. However, this challenge is an opportunity in disguise, and DAOs should seek alternative ways to identify, encourage and empower contributions from participants. DAOs can use alternative processes such as voting, work distribution, and idea crowdsourcing to guide decision-making in place of a formal hierarchy."

- Organize for empowerment: "A clear mission is an important safeguard to help participants make decisions aligned with a DAO's intended outcomes. To make up for the lack of hierarchy, DAOs can organize in a way that empowers participant action. Establishing clear areas of responsibility and need is an effective way to help participants assess their ability to contribute based on their skills and expertise."

- Explore legal structures and risks: "There is no formal legal entity for a DAO. Still, participants should seek to understand the legal structures available based on the

---

DAO's types of activity. There is a vibrant community of thought leaders exploring alternative entity structures, and DAOs should stay up-to-date with the latest developments. DAO participants should articulate the activity they will engage in and seek legal counsel to understand legal and financial risks."

- Learn from the DAO community: "As the concept of a DAO evolves, participants should seek to connect with other DAOs to share and learn best practices from the web3 community." .

DAO Services

To help with the creation and management of DAOs, there are new services to streamline the process. These are usually traditional SaaS tools.

For example, there is Poko, which is startup backed by YCombinator. The company's platform can set up the basic structure of a DAO within a couple minutes. It handles such things as:

- Legal Infrastructure: Poko is focused on helping the DAO engage in real-life interactions with the law. This is done with both on-chain and off-chain assets.

- Governance: Poko has templates to allow for creating voting rights that are fair. But this is also done in a way that provides for a process that does not get bogged down.

- Fundraising: The platform helps with this. In fact, it is built for large asset raises. One of the founders, Geoffrey See, was the Chief Strategy Officer and founding team member of Zilliqa. The protocol reached $2 billion.[9]

Another interesting service provider is Opolis. This helps to provide traditional employee benefits for DAOs like payroll, health insurance, 401(k) plans, and so on. To do this, Opolis has created an employment cooperative. This has allowed for getting more discounts because of the scale of the organization.

In May 2021, Opolis raised $5 million. Note that many of the investors were DAOs, DeFI projects, and investment syndicates. Examples included BadgerDAO, MakerDAO Foundation, and MetaPurse.

---

[9] www.ycombinator.com/companies/poko

According to John Paller, Executive Steward of Opolis: "We set out to demonstrate that 'communities funding communities' is the new norm for early-stage funding of key infrastructural projects in Web3. Gathering investors and funders whose long-term goals are in alignment with that of other ecosystem stakeholders was top priority for us."[10]

Public Benefit Corporations

A traditional corporation has a clear-cut goal. It's about benefiting the shareholders. It's really that simple.

But over the years, many entrepreneurs have soured on this concept. They instead believe there are multiple stakeholders to focus on, such as employees, the customers, partners, and even the environment.

Historically, Wall Street has generally been resistant to this. But there has actually been notable change lately. More investors are starting to look at principles like ESG (Environment, Social, and Governance).

Take a look at Larry Fink. He is the CEO and cofounder of BlackRock, which is one of the world's largest asset managers. In his 2022 annual report to shareholders, he defended ESG and encouraged corporations to focus on stakeholders beyond the shareholders.[11]

Consider that there is actually a new type of corporation emerging – called the public benefit corporation – that has the goal to focus on these ESG values. It is becoming more popular with Web3 startups.

Keep in mind that the public benefit corporation is recognized in Delaware, which is the leading jurisdiction for corporate law. The specification is part of a company's certificate of incorporation.

Some companies are also electing for the Certified B Corp status. This essentially is about providing more accountability and transparency for the ESG goals. This is accomplished by using the criteria of third-party nonprofit organizations like B Lab.

An example of a Web3 company that is a public benefit corporation is Optimism. Here's how the company describes it: "Not only are we writing software that scales Ethereum technology, we are also scaling Ethereum values by creating the rails for highly impactful projects that don't have a

---

[10] www.globenewswire.com/news-release/2021/05/12/2228012/0/en/Opolis-Inc-Trustee-to-the-Employment-Commons-completes-4-75M-Communities-Funding-Communities-funding-round.html

[11] www.nytimes.com/2022/01/18/business/dealbook/fink-blackrock-woke.html

business model to succeed…Until the project is fully decentralized, we will be donating all profits from running a centralized sequencer towards scaling and sustaining public goods."[12]

Now as for the rest of the chapter, we'll take a look at some of the interesting DAOs and how they operate.

MakerDAO

While studying at the University of Copenhagen and Copenhagen Business School, Rune Christensen ran a startup. It focused on having Westerners teach English to persons in China.

But when Christensen learned about blockchain and Bitcoin in 2011, he sold his startup. He also put much of his money into crypto.

However, he realized there were problems with the industry, such as the breaches. Bitcoin also was highly volatile. So, this is why Christensen invented a stablecoin – called DAI – and it became part of one of the first DAOs: MakerDAO.[13] He built this on the Ethereum network.

The timing was certainly on target. From the start, MakerDAO became quite popular – and it remains one of the world's largest DAOs.

But there were some tough times. In early 2020, MakerDAO suffered major losses because of the plunge in Ether. But Christensen would adapt to this and turn Dai into a stablecoin with various forms of collateral. Within a few months, this would turn into the first DeFI protocol to exceed $1 billion.[14]

MakerDAO has been diversifying its platform into traditional loans. A notable example is one of the DAO's clients, 6s Capital, a commercial lender. The company used the MakerDAO technology to structure a $7.8 million loan to Tesla for the financing of new repair and collision centers.[15]

Friends with Benefits

Trevor McFedries' career started in the music industry. He was a musician who signed a contract with Interscope while he was in his early 20s.

---

[12] www.optimism.io/about
[13] www.linkedin.com/in/runebentsenchristensen/?originalSubdomain=dk
[14] https://cointelegraph.com/top-people-in-crypto-and-blockchain-2021/rune-christensen
[15] https://thedefiant.io/tesla-makerdao-loan/

But he had another important talent: he could code. This would eventually land him a job at Spotify in 2010.[16] The role for McFedries was to help make the streaming service mainstream.

When he discovered crypto and Ethereum, he saw an opportunity to revolutionize the entertainment industry. He then went on to create the Friends with Benefits (F.W.B.) DAO.

His community-building skills were definitely essential. In little time, he built F.W.B. into a thriving platform. He also created the first social token, which was $FWB.

Think of F.W.B. as a modern-day forum for creatives. To join, you need to buy the token, which gives you access to the V.I.P. lounge. You can then communicate with the users via Discord. But there are also in-person meetups. By doing this, the community can create content – such as music, movies, and so on.

According to a blog from Andreessen Horowitz, which is an investor in the DAO: "By aligning the incentives of the next generation of artists, creators, and builders, FWB is enabling a different kind of renaissance for the next evolution of the internet. Fittingly, they describe themselves as a digital city."[17]

SailGP

Larry Ellison, the cofounder and chief technology officer of Oracle, is a long-time sailing enthusiast. His team has won two America's Cups.

In 2019, Ellison created SailGP, which is an international racing series. It uses the F50 catamarans.

While Ellison is one of the wealthiest persons in the world, he still likes to find ways to help finance his ventures. The same goes for SailGP. To this end, he teamed up with Near Protocol to make a DAO for it.[18]

By doing this, the fans will have a way to participate. This could be by deciding on the lineup, the branding, and even strategies.

According to the SailGP website: "Our ambition is to give fans the opportunity to own exclusive SailGP NFT moments and artwork, giving access to previously unavailable content and making you part of a community this is at the forefront of sports and technology."[19]

---

[16] https://consensys.net/blog/codefi/friends-with-benefits-a-new-model-for-social-tokens-on-ethereum/

[17] https://a16z.com/2021/10/27/investing-in-friends-with-benefits-a-dao/

[18] www.ledgerinsights.com/larry-ellisons-sailgp-to-launch-sports-team-dao/

[19] https://sailgp.com/general/near/

Uniswap

In the summer of 2017, Siemens laid off Hayden Adams, who was a mechanical engineer.[20] But this turned out to be a very good thing. Adams delved into blockchain and Ethereum. He then received a $65,000 grant from the Ethereum Foundation.[21]

Adams created the Uniswap protocol and DAO. At first, he used the Solidity language. But he realized that Vyper would be a better option to create sophisticated smart contracts.

Uniswap would become the basis for the largest decentralized and automated market system to trade on the Ethereum platform. The governance token is UNI, which was launched in late 2020. In a sense, Uniswap became a new kind of financial market – in which the users decided on its fate.

The voting structure for technical proposals is as follows:

- Temperature Check: There needs to be a minimum level of interest in the new feature. This requires at least 25,000 UNI votes.

- Consensus Check: This is where the proposer makes a formal specification for the new function. For this, there must be a minimum of 50,000 UNI yes votes.

- Final Phase: The proposer will provide audited codes. For this, there needs to be 40 million UNI yes votes.

As of early 2022, Uniswap had over $924 billion in trading volume and more than 94 million trades.[22]

Conclusion

A DAO is the main way to provide decentralized governance for a Web3 organization. This allows for proposing and voting on various matters. To participate in this, a user will buy tokens.

DAOs are a relatively new concept, and the legal implications are far from clear. But there are emerging core best practices. Some states and countries are also providing legal structures for DAOs.

---

[20] https://medium.com/@darrenmims22/uniswap-the-story-b1239af6427b
[21] www.coindesk.com/markets/2020/12/08/hayden-adams-king-of-the-defi-degens/
[22] https://uniswap.org/

Despite this, it's common for there to be a hybrid legal approach. This means having a traditional corporate wrapper for the DAO.

But there are also downsides to DAOs. Let's face it, it's tough to anticipate potential issues by using smart contracts. The set up can be complex and expensive. Then there are the potential issues with the creators of the DAO, who may have conflicts of interest.

Regardless, DAOs have become quite popular. And over time, there will certainly be progress in dealing with the issues.

As for the next chapter, we'll take a look at startups for NFTs and gaming.

NFTs, Gaming, and Social Networks

The Consumer Startup

Mike Winkelmann is a graphic designer and artist.[1] He is better known as Beeple. He has been an innovator, using technologies like Virtual Reality (VR) and Augmented Reality (AR) for his artwork. Beeple has also been a go-to person for many celebrities. Just some examples include Nicki Minaj, Eminem, Justin Bieber, One Direction, and Katy Perry.

In 2020, Beeple started to explore non-fungible tokens (NFTs). This a technology, which is based on blockchain, that allows people to own digital items.

---

[1] www.beeple-crap.com/about

© Tom Taulli 2022
T. Taulli, *How to Create a Web3 Startup*,
https://doi.org/10.1007/978-1-4842-8683-8_6

He started to create digital art with NFTs, and they were fetching thousands of dollars. But all this would pale in comparison to his digital collage of political cartoons and video game images, called "Everydays: The First 5,000 Days."

He put this up for auction at Christie's and the bidding was intense (there were 353 bids). The winner would pay a hefty $69.3 million for the NFT. It was the third most paid for any living artist, behind Jeff Koons and David Hockney.[2]

No doubt, the auction caused a stir – and it was a catalyst for enormous growth in the NFT market. It was also one of the first Web3 consumer applications that became mainstream.

But of course, there are others as well. Web3 gaming and social networks have seen lots of traction as well.

In this chapter, we'll see how these markets are developing and the opportunities for entrepreneurs.

How Do NFTs Work?

Until the creation of NFTs, it was not possible to own digital items. After all, a person could just copy and paste it, right? Definitely. It's why content industries, such as for music have struggled in the digital world.

But NFTs would be a game changer. By using the blockchain, it was possible to provide a unique token for the digital item.

The first NFT came out in 2017. A studio, called Larva Labs, developed digital characters called CryptoPunks.[3] The company essentially made it possible to trade them, such as you would with a traditional collectible.

NFTs are generally built on the Ethereum blockchain and use the ERC-721 protocol. This allows for storing various details. All this is transparent to the public. And an NFT can be virtually for anything.

As should be no surprise, there can be some confusion with NFTs. Keep in mind that it does not convey any copyrights. They still belong to whoever owns the physical item. For example, there may be an NFT for the Mona Lisa. But this does not mean you own the original painting.

---

[2]www.wsj.com/articles/beeple-nft-fetches-record-breaking-69-million-in-christies-sale-11615477732?mod=article_inline
[3]www.nationalworld.com/lifestyle/money/nft-meaning-crypto-art-tech-explained-what-is-a-non-fungible-token-where-to-buy-them-and-best-marketplace-3163733

> **Note**   Quentin Tarantino, the scriptwriter of the iconic film "Pulp Fiction," attempted to create NFTs for seven exclusive scenes.[4] But the studio that produced the film, Miramax, filed a lawsuit to prevent this. It's far from clear what the outcome will be. But the case could prove critical in setting forth the rights for NFTs.

Next, an NFT is not a cryptocurrency. The main reason is that a cryptocurrency is fungible. For example, a Bitcoin is no different from another one. You can easily exchange them. A non-fungible token, however, is nontransferable. None are alike. Although, you can use a cryptocurrency to acquire an NFT.

NFTs and cryptocurrencies rely on the same underlying blockchain technology. NFT marketplaces may also require people to purchase NFTs with a cryptocurrency. However, cryptocurrencies and NFTs are created and used for different purposes.

Note that the NFT market has posted a staggering growth. In 2021, the spending came to $17.6 billion, up by about 21,000%.[5]

Here are some other interesting facts:

- NFT investors made roughly $5.4 billion in profits.
- There are 2.2 million wallets for NFT transactions.
- More than 470 wallets have over $1 million in NFTS.

By far, the most popular category was for collectibles. But there was also strong growth with gaming and the Metaverse.

However, by 2022, the NFT market would look much different. The growth rates plummeted as the crypto market came under tremendous pressure. Yet the levels of activity were still much higher than a few years earlier.

> **Note**   While many NFTs are stored on the Ethereum network, there are certainly alternatives. Some of the more notable ones include Flow and Tezos.

---

[4] https://deadline.com/2021/12/quentin-tarantino-nft-lawsuit-dismissal-motion-pulp-fiction-miramax-1234888031/
[5] www.cnbc.com/2022/03/10/trading-in-nfts-spiked-21000percent-to-top-17-billion-in-2021-report.html#:~:text=Trading%20in%20nonfungible%20tokens%20hit,increasingly%20warming%20to%20the%20market

Examples of NFTs

The music streaming industry has become a massive global business. For example, Spotify has 180 million paid subscribers and 406 million monthly active users (MAUs).[6] The service is available in 183 markets.

Despite this, the rewards for the musicians is far from attractive. Consider that Spotify has eight million musicians on its platform and only about 14,000 make $50,000 or more per year.[7] In other words, many of them cannot make a living from this channel.

But this is where NFTs can make a difference. It is a way for musicians – or any creators – to better monetize their art. They can often keep more than 95% of the revenues.

True, if creators do not use a platform like Spotify, they will not have the enormous scale. But in the Web3 world, you do not need large numbers. Rather, it's more about catering to your avid fans. They will likely be willing to spend more money, such as through the use of NFTs. This can also be an effective way for the creators to build even stronger connections with their fans.

Take the example of the band, Kings of Leon. In early 2021, they released their new album as an NFT. It was the first time that this had been done.

The band provided three types of tokens.[8] They provided different perks, whether VIP seats, exclusive art, and so on.

The band raised over $2 million from its NFT offering.[9] About $500,000 was a donation to Live Nation's Crew Nation, which helped music crews during the COVID-19 pandemic.

This is not to imply that it is easy to make money from NFTs. It's not. The fact is that you will still need to rely on marketing, say with a following on Instagram, Facebook, or Twitter. These are still very effective channels for super fans.

Just take a look at the interesting case with Brandon Sanderson, a top fantasy writer of series like "Mistborn." In 2022, he set up a Kickstarter campaign. It had different tiers for his readers that included access to four upcoming novels, and monthly subscription boxes.

---

[6] https://investors.spotify.com/home/default.aspx

[7] www.theverge.com/23020727/decoder-chris-dixon-web3-crypto-a16z-vc-silicon-valley-investing-podcast-interview

[8] www.rollingstone.com/pro/news/kings-of-leon-when-you-see-yourself-album-nft-crypto-1135192/

[9] www.nme.com/news/music/kings-of-leon-have-generated-2million-from-nft-sales-of-their-new-album-2899349

Well, it was a huge success. In all, Sanderson raised $41.7 million.[10]

It definitely highlighted the power of crowdfunding. But it also showed the importance of traditional publishers like Tor. Let's face it, this helped Sanderson build up a loyal following – which he developed since he started publishing his works in 2003.

Buying and Creating NFTs

Buying an NFT can be cumbersome. And this is one of the drawbacks of the market. Although, the process will inevitably get better.

The first step in buying an NFT is getting the right token for the transaction. Often this is ether. You can get this from a crypto exchange like Coinbase.

Next, you need to transfer your cryptocurrency to a wallet and a common one is MetaMask. Then you will need to connect your wallet to an NFT marketplace. Here are some examples:

- OpenSea
- NBA Top Shot
- CrytpoPunks
- Rarible
- Foundation
- Binance NFT
- Nifty Gateway
- Mintable

You will search around the marketplace. When you find an NFT that you like, you will then make a purchase. There may also be an auction for it. Regardless, the NFT will be in your wallet, and you can sell it in the future, such as on a marketplace.

OK then, so how do you create an NFT? Of course, you will need to specify an item that it will represent. Again, this can be just about anything. But the item should be something that you have a right to. If not, you could be violating the copyright laws and you may potentially be liable for damages.

---

[10] www.engadget.com/brandon-sanderson-kickstarter-campaign-record-most-funded-091530765.html

You will then select the type of blockchain. Usually, this is Ethereum. Next, you will need to set up your digital wallet and then buy cryptocurrency. You will then select the NFT marketplace and make the connection to your wallet. You will upload the digital file, such as a GIF, PNG, or MP3.

You'll decide on how to sell your NFT. The options include the following:

- Fixed price

- A timed auction

- Unlimited auction. This means you can end it when you want

If you have an auction, you will set a minimum price as well as the royalty levels (this is for subsequent sales on secondary markets). However, the fees can be significant, such as with the gas for Ethereum. It's actually common to lose money on NFT sales because of this.

The Value of NFTs

As is the case with cryptocurrencies, it's difficult to value NFTs. It's generally a subjective process.

Yet there are some guidelines to consider. Here's a look:

- Rarity: Scarcity can create value. It certainly helps that NFTs are unique. But of course, this is little help if there is not much interest in the digital item. This is why it's typical that a valuable NFT – especially when it comes to art and entertainment – is something that is exclusive or different. This was definitely the case with Beeple.

- Utility: This is usually for digital items that are not art. Basically, utility means that you can do something with the NFT. An example would be one that allows you to get into a concert (although, such as NFT may have limited value because there will likely be a time limit). Another case is where you can use it as a way to make purchases in a game or the Metaverse.

- Tangibility: This is when the NFT has a connection to the physical world. An example is real estate. A token can represent fractional ownership. This can help with recordkeeping and reducing the potential for fraud.

- Provenance: This is a history of who has owned the NFT. This can provide insight on the value of the item. After all, the prior owners may have a good track record with NFTs.

- Liquidity: Looking at the blockchain, has the NFT seen continued interest from buyers? What has been the demand for similar digital items?

- Social Proof: This describes where a celebrity is backing the NFT. True, this is not guaranteed to create value. But it is still a very important factor to consider.

- Interoperability: This means you can use the NFT for other platforms. For example, you could buy NFTs on one game, but use it for another one.

Problems for NFTs

Sina Estavi is the CEO of Bridge Oracle, which is a blockchain company based in Malaysia. In 2021, he agreed to pay $2.9 million for the NFT from Jack Dorsey (he donated the money to charity). It was for the first tweet on Twitter, which was "just setting up my twttr."

The purchase caused a stir – and helped to propel even more interest in the NFT market.

But unfortunately, things did not turn out too well for Estavi. Within less than a year, he put up the NFT for bid – and there was tepid interest. The bids did not even exceed $14,000.[11]

Such an outcome is not unusual. The reality is that the NFT market is highly volatile – even more so than cryptocurrencies.

If anything, the values are often subject to speculation. There is also the impact of fads.

It's true that you can still make lots of money from NFTs, but you probably need to take a shorter-term focus. Success may be more like day trading.

---

[11] www.wsj.com/articles/jack-dorsey-tweet-nft-once-sold-for-2-9-million-now-might-fetch-under-14-000-11650110402?mod=hp_featst_pos3

Yet there are other nagging issues with the NFT market:

- Adoption: As seen earlier in this chapter, the process for buying and creating NFTs is far from intuitive. But if the market is to become more mainstream, there must be significant improvement. There will essentially need to be one-click transactions like Amazon.

- Rug Pulls: This is where a Web3 developer abandons a project and takes the money. There can be little recourse for those who have been defrauded.

- Whitelisting: This is where a select group of people are invited to participate in a project. Then when it is launched to the public, they will derive significant gains. This is similar to the "pump and dump" of penny stocks. According to research from Chainalysis, whitelisted users made 75% gains, while the general users got only 20%.[12] Unfortunately, this is a common practice, and it can be difficult to do anything about it.

- Wash Trading: A user is both the seller and buyer for a transaction. This is possible because you can easily create two wallets and not provide any identifying information. With wash trading, this can cause artificial volume in an NFT, which may attract interest.

- Copyright Violations: It's not difficult for someone to create an NFT from someone else's intellectual property. This not only defrauds the real owner but also the user who makes the purchase.

New Go-to-Market Strategies

In 2010, Kevin Systrom and Mike Krieger created an app called Burbn. It allowed users to check-in to locations and post messages and photos. But there was a problem: It got little traction. The application was clunky – which was common for the early days of iOS apps – and had little utility.

---

[12] www.nytimes.com/interactive/2022/03/18/technology/nft-guide.html

But Systrom and Kreiger noticed something interesting. Burbn users really liked the photo sharing feature. So the founders just focused on this and created Instagram.[13] It also had the ability to edit the photos. Although, perhaps the most important feature was that it only took three clicks to post a photo.

Within a month, Instagram got over one million users.[14] There was also no advertising or marketing. The growth was purely word-of-mouth.

Within two years, the founders sold Instagram to Facebook for $1 billion.

This is certainly another iconic Silicon Valley story. But this was also a very rare success. For the most part, startups usually need significant marketing. This is where a large part of the venture capital goes.

Then with Web3, might things be different? Will there be less need for venture capital?

Perhaps so. The reason is that Web3's focus on tokens can act as a financing mechanism. It can also be an effective way to attract users. Hey, who doesn't want to get paid, right?

But with Web3, the typical evolution of a startup is usually different. You can start without a product. Instead, you will set forth the idea for one and then you will get the feedback from the community that owns tokens. This helps to provide for the product-market fit.

But to make this happen, there will need to be a compelling vision. What will encourage people to come on board and make a bet on your venture? What problems are you looking to solve?

By answering these questions, you will have a better chance of creating a strong community. They will also have better direction on providing the feedback to improve on the vision.

In terms of go-to-market strategies, there are a variety of interesting ones emerging. Here's a look at some of them:

- Developer Grants: This is a way to encourage coders to come on board the project. The grant could be in the form of tokens or traditional money. Regardless, there is usually a need for some type of incentive to get interest. For example, Compound set up a developer grant program from March 12 to September 12, 2022, and

---

[13] www.theatlantic.com/technology/archive/2014/07/instagram-used-to-be-called-brbn/373815/
[14] www.bbc.com/news/technology-45640386

funded it with 5,000 of its own tokens, COMP.[15] According to the website: "With no carrot with which to motivate community members to propose changes, the protocol isn't able to innovate as quickly as it should be innovating in a dynamic and competitive market." The program is not just for development of new features. It also provides for code audits, and bounties for finding bugs.

- Memes: These can help create viral growth in the user base. Although, creating memes is no easy feat. The founders may also not be the best ones to do this. Instead, this is really for those with a marketing background. It also helps to have a large following on traditional social media channels. And something else to keep in mind: The impact of memes tends to be temporary. In other words, the creation of them is likely something to be ongoing.

- Airdrops: This is when a Web3 project gives away tokens. It's also possible to airdrop NFTs. Often, this is to encourage people to sign up for a project. But it also can be used for testing the project's technology. A famous example of an NFT airdrop is the Bored Ape Yacht Club. The project created a new collection, called the Mutant Ape Yacht Club. There was an airdrop that gave all existing users the ability to create 10,000 apes, which were referred to as "mutants." There was also another 10,000 available for new users. This was a fun reward for existing users. But it was also an effective way to bring new ones.

Social Identity of Web3

In the Web3 world, it's common for users to have their own avatars. They can also serve as profile pictures for social media. They are often old-school, retrograde pixelated visuals, such as of punks or bored apes. For example, Jay-Z and Snoop Dogg have these on their Twitter and Instagram accounts.

The concept behind Web3 profile photos is that they should not be polished. Rather, what's important is the engagement with the community.

---

[15] https://compoundgrants.org/what-is-the-program

Keep in mind that many of the profiles are NFTs. By doing this, they can become a next-generation version of a resume. Since the NFTs are on a blockchain, a user can get a public view of the activities of the users.

The Web3 Social Network

By the end of 2021, Facebook's user base reached 2.82 billion users, up 8% on a year-over-year basis.[16] At the time, there were close to eight billion people in the world.

Facebook has definitely done a great job in monetizing this. The 2021 revenues were a massive $117.9 billion, and the profits came to $39.3 billion.

But for those people who contributed content to Facebook, how much did it pay out? Basically, very little. The reason is that much of the company's revenues come from advertising.

There is nothing wrong with this. Many people enjoy Facebook. It's not about making a buck.

Yet for Web3 entrepreneurs, they are looking to upend Facebook's model. And the blockchain means that users will have more control over their data and have the opportunity to earn tokens.

The Web3 social network is likely to look very different from a traditional platform. First of all, the interface may use open-source tools, such as for the chat. Or it could be based on a proprietary system like Discord.

Next, a Web3 social network is likely to be much smaller than a Twitter, Snap, or Facebook. The reason is that there will be a focus on a particular community. Part of the reason for this is there will likely be a DAO involved. For this, there will be a specific purpose. If not, it could be difficult to attract the right people to make the social network engaging.

Now a key advantage of a Web3 social network is the portability. If you want to leave, you will not be giving up your social graph and content. It belongs to you, as it is on the blockchain, and you maintain the data through your ownership of the hash. You can then transfer this to another platform.

By contrast, a traditional social network is a walled garden. When you leave, you cannot transfer your users or content. It still belongs to the social network, unless you delete the account or turn it off.

---

[16] https://investor.fb.com/investor-news/press-release-details/2022/Meta-Reports-Fourth-Quarter-and-Full-Year-2021-Results/default.aspx

This has been a huge source of power for social networks. It's why that – when there are violations of privacy or other major problems – there is often little impact on the user numbers. The users are essentially locked in.

As a result, social networks have significant power, such as changing policies. If Twitter no longer wants something on its platform, it can simply prohibit it. Or if it wants to charge the fees, it can do so.

This is also the case with large online marketplaces. Just look at iOS. If you want to publish an app on the platform, you need to go through a review process. If you fail, it could be a big setback for an entrepreneur.

Then there are the fees. Apple generally charges 30% on the revenues generated from apps. All in all, this can make it difficult for entrepreneurs to make money. This is even the case for the largest tech companies. Note that game maker Epic is suing Apple over its Appstore policies.

Web3 social networks are still in the nascent stages. There has yet to be one that has been a breakout. But this will certainly change – and probably soon.

Here are some interesting startups in the space:

- APPICS: The founder is Uma Hagenguth, who is based in Switzerland. She started her first business at age 16, with a focus on marketing and web design.[17] As for crypto, she got started with this in 2013. Her idea for APPICS is to create a rewards-based social network with a sleek interface. Users can earn tokens by creating content that generates certain numbers of likes and comments.[18] Thus, the incentives are based on engagement. APPICS is built on the Telos blockchain. The app is available on iOS and Google Play.

- Aave: This is another startup in Switzerland. The founder, Stani Kulechov, launched it in 2017.[19] He started it while as a law student in Helsinki. The company is one of the early developers of a DeFi cryptocurrency (based on the Ethereum network). But Aave is also moving into the social media space. The project is called the Lens Protocol

---

[17] www.linkedin.com/in/uma-hagenguth/?originalSubdomain=ch
[18] https://cointelegraph.com/news/web3-social-media-app-that-rewards-creators-with-crypto-goes-live-on-app-store
[19] www.kraken.com/en-us/learn/what-is-aave-lend

and is based on the Polygon blockchain.[20] This allows for the creation of a user profile that is an NFT, which contains all the social media content. The user can decide how to monetize this. Interestingly enough, Aave is exploring the idea of turning profiles into DAOs.

- Yup: This is a Web3 platform that allows people to curate content from platforms like OpenSea, Twitter, YouTube, and Mirror. Yup pays its users based on engagement. In early 2022, the company raised $3.5 million from Distributed Global.[21]

Web3 Gaming

An early success story in Web3 is gaming. The category is often called GameFi or crypto gaming.

According to a report from DappRadar x BGA Games, the growth in the market was a sizzling 2,000% for the first quarter of 2022.[22] About 52% of all blockchain activity was due to gaming. There were about 1.22 million wallets.

Venture funding has accelerated. In the first quarter of 2022, the investments came to about $2.5 billion[23] and the estimate is that it could be $10 billion for the year.

A notable deal was for Animoca Brands, which is a startup based in Melbourne, Australia. The company raised $359 million at a pre-money valuation of over $5 billion.[24] The lead investor was Liberty City Ventures.

Animoca Brands has developed various centralized and decentralized games. They are also for mobile, game consoles, PCs, and web. The company has been a pioneer of using blockchain for in-game rewards and monetization.

The traction in Web3 gaming should not be surprising. Many gamers are already familiar with blockchain and crypto. Besides, the gaming industry has been an early adopter of allowing the purchase of virtual items.

---

[20] https://cointelegraph.com/news/aave-launches-web3-social-media-platform-lens-protocol
[21] https://crypto.news/web3-social-media-platform-yup-3-6-million-funding/
[22] www.coindesk.com/tech/2022/04/20/blockchain-gaming-usage-explodes-2000-in-a-year-dappradar/
[23] https://decrypt.co/98263/investors-poured-2-5b-crypto-games-q1-2022-report
[24] www.animocabrands.com/animoca-brands-raises-usd358888888-at-usd5b-valuation-to-grow-the-open-metaverse

In the years ahead, gaming will likely be how a large number of people will initially participate in Web3. This will accelerate as it gets easier to onboard users.

Yet the traditional game industry has had challenges with microtransactions. Simply put, it has been difficult to make this affordable with the legacy financial services infrastructure.

But blockchain and crypto should change this. It will allow for a more efficient approach. There will also be a benefit for gamers to control their tokens. This can mean that they can spend it elsewhere. This makes it more compelling for gamers to participate.

Note   There are emerging gaming marketplaces like Tegro. They are focused on providing a way for gamers to buy and sell their virtual items.

By comparison, with a traditional game, there is the risk of losing virtual assets. The reason is that there is a central authority that essentially owns everything. When a game shuts down, the gamers will likely lose their holdings. It's happened with titles like Minecraft Earth and Harry Potter Wizards Unite.

Another interesting aspect of Web3 gaming is the community involvement. By setting up a DAO, it's possible for the users to decide on the rules and evolution of the game. This can further add to the engagement and fun. However, for the game developer, it's important to not get too carried away. If there is too much decision-making, this can bog down the game. There needs to be a balance.

An interesting aspect of Web3 community is the notion of exclusivity. For example, you can show that you were one of the original players of a game. And in the community, this could certainly confer some status.

There is also the opportunity for Web3 games to create lasting brands. They can evolve with the help of the users as well. All this may ultimately mean that Web3 games will lead to next-generation entertainment companies, which could ultimately rival traditional studios like Marvel.

For a Web3 gaming startup, the initial offering may not even begin as a game. It could be a blog, a collection of NFTs, or a content site. This would have an interesting story line that gains interest from users. From this, a startup can then put together a game around it. All along, the community will be a part of the world-building process.

But there are certain factors that will not change when it comes to Web3 gaming. After all, a game needs to be standout. The reality is that the market will get quickly saturated and it will be more difficult to rise above the noise. This means there will be a need for more resources to be invested in the games – but also a good amount of creativity, which is something that is not easy to pull off.

Another issue is that the gaming industry is subject to fads. A hot game can quickly go very cold. It's very rare for there to be one that lasts for a few years. But with the crypto mechanics, this is something that is necessary. It is what builds real value.

Even successful gaming companies can languish. An example of this is Zynga. In 2012, the company had a high-profile IPO, with the stock price at $10. But the business would come under pressure. Zynga then went on to spend billions on acquisitions, but this really did not move the needle. In early 2022, Zynga sold out to Take-Two Interactive.[25] What did investors get? Well, it was $9.86 per share.

With Web3, it's critical to understand economics. An entrepreneur may even want to bring on board an economist! Why so? The reason is that a Web3 game will be a true economic system, with supply and demand for tokens. However, if this is not structured properly, the game could easily fall apart. In some cases, it may look more like a Ponzi scheme or multi-level marketing ploy. This is where the benefits for the early users start to dwindle because new members are not being brought into the ecosystem. When this happens, the users may want to leave because the value of their tokens will have depreciated significantly.

What's more, the economics of a Web3 game can mean that it can cost thousands of dollars to play. Of course, this may not be possible for many users. To deal with this, there are guilds that pool resources to allow for the playing of the game. Another option is to have a trial period.

A popular business model for Web3 is play-to-earn. The innovator of this approach is Sky Mavis, which is based in Vietnam. The company is the developer of the Axie Infinity game.

Here's how it works: The players breed the characters, which are referred to as Axies. They can then engage in fights and adventures. But there is also an economy. The players, for example, can acquire land, create potions, and so on. To handle these transactions, the games allow for the trading of NFTs – which represent ownership in the virtual items – and ether. The Axie Infinity native token is AXS.

---

[25] www.marketwatch.com/story/after-billions-in-acquisitions-zynga-still-sells-for-less-than-ipo-price-11641841386

The transactions in the marketplace have reached $3.6 billion and the highest price paid for an Axie was for $820,000.[26] There are 2.8 million daily active players.

 Note   Some of the most popular play-to-earn games include Splinterlands, Alien Worlds, and Decentralized.

Andreessen Horowitz is an investor in Sky Mavis. In a blog post, the authors noted: "What Axie Infinity has unlocked is the ability to play the games you love, have fun, but also participate in the financial upside of the community. This is an incredibly powerful idea: it means that games are no longer pure entertainment, but cross over into the realm of work. Axie Infinity is transforming communities around the world and replacing traditional forms of employment, changing people's lives as players of the game help each other succeed."[27]

Another business model for Web3 games is play-to-own. This is similar to play-to-earn, as both approaches involve providing incentives with crypto and tokens.

So, what's the difference? It's more about degree. With play-to-earn, this usually has higher financial rewards. It's actually possible for some people to make a living with the game.

A play-to-own game, on the other hand, is more about the fun and engagement. Making money is rather a nice bonus.

A popular play-to-own game is Crypto Raiders. It's about dungeon crawling, in which the players can use crypto to buy characters, mobs, missions, and so on. The platform is built on the Polygon blockchain.

In March 2022, Crypto Raiders raised $6 million. The lead investors included DeFiance Capital and Delphi Digital.

Crypto Raiders CEO and cofounder, Nicholas Kneuper, noted: "We built Crypto Raiders with the RPG games we played growing up in mind. Those games are the perfect use case to bring together gaming and the blockchain."[28]

Finally, there is the move-to-earn model. It's focused on the physical world and promotes wellness. How so? Take a look at the top operator in the

---

[26] https://axieinfinity.com/
[27] https://a16z.com/2021/10/05/investing-in-axie-infinity/
[28] www.businesswire.com/news/home/20220330005225/en/ Emerging-NFT-Role-Playing-Game-RPG-Crypto-Raiders-Scores-6-Million-in-Funding-From-DeFiance-Capital-Delphi-Digital-and-Others

market: STEPN. To play this game, you purchase NFTs, which are based on the Solana blockchain. Then you track your movements with the GPS on your smartphone. By doing this, you get in-app token rewards. The bottom line: This is a way to promote more healthy living.

In 2022, STEPN announced a $5 million seed funding.[29] The lead investors included Sequoia Capital India and Folius Ventures.

Brands and NFTs

Because of privacy regulations, it is getting tougher for companies to use digital platforms to connect with their customers. Consider the use of cookies. These allow for the tracking of user behavior. It has also made it possible to use retargeting of ads. But cookies are on their way out. Google's Chrome will sunset them in 2023. The same goes for Firefox and Safari.

Or look at the new privacy requirements from Apple. For iOS apps, they require that users opt-in for tracking. And as should be no surprise, this has had an adverse impact on online marketing efforts. Facebook noted that it will reduce 2022 sales by more than $10 billion.[30]

In light of this, advertisers are looking for alternatives. Interestingly enough, NFTs may be a big help. This is done by using existing or new content. This can then include incentives, perks, and discounts.

In fact, this strategy can allow a company to have more control over its online domain. Let's face it, when relying on platforms like Facebook, YouTube, TikTok, or Twitter, there is the possible adverse impact of a change in an algorithm. This could reduce the impact of the advertising or could mean that the advertiser will need to pay more.

Yet there needs to be caution. When it comes to the Web3 world, the users usually do not want blatant marketing pitches. They instead prefer engaging content, and immersive experiences that enhance a company's product or service. This may also include providing assistance for a cause, such as by donating funds to a nonprofit.

Here are some examples:

- For the 95th anniversary of the Macy's Thanksgiving Day Parade, the company auctioned ten NFTs.[31] They each had a parade balloon from prior events. The proceeds

---

[29] www.theblockcrypto.com/post/130953/solana-move-to-earn-stepn-funding
[30] www.wsj.com/articles/facebook-feels-10-billion-sting-from-apples-privacy-push-11643898139
[31] www.theverge.com/2021/11/24/22800985/macys-thanksgiving-day-parade-nfts-auction

from the auction went to the Make-A-Wish Foundation. The company also gave away 9,500 NFTs to people who signed up.

- For the 40th anniversary of McDonald's McRib, the company gave away a limited-edition NFT.[32] To get this, people had to follow @McDonalds on Twitter and retweet the Sweepstakes Invitation.

- Mattel launched the Hot Wheels NFT Garage. This involved a series of 40 new NFTs for the iconic toy cars.[33] There was also a promotion to win limited-edition die-cast vehicles.

As a validation of this market, look at Nike. In late 2021, the company agreed to acquire RTFKT, an NFT studio for creating crypto collectibles. This startup was the partner of CloneX, which was involved in the creation of a highly successful NFT called CryptoSlam. It generated over $65 million in transactions.[34]

In the press release for the deal, Nike CEO John Donahoe said: "This acquisition is another step that accelerates Nike's digital transformation and allows us to serve athletes and creators at the intersection of sport, creativity, gaming and culture."[35]

OK then, as for the rest of the chapter, we'll take a look at some of the interesting other startups in the NFT space.

Novel

Roger Beaman is a software engineer who has worked at Goldman Sachs and Shutterstock.[36] In 2021, he co-founded Novel. The goal was to make it easier for companies to create, buy, and sell NFTs. It would be similiar to using a platform like Shopify. Beaman would go on to raise $6 million for his startup.[37]

---

[32] www.prnewswire.com/news-releases/mcdonalds-usa-unveils-first-ever-nft-to-celebrate-40th-anniversary-of-the-mcrib-301410515.html
[33] www.businesswire.com/news/home/20211026006314/en/Mattel-Partners-with-WAX-to-Release-Hot-Wheels-NFT-Garage---Series-1
[34] https://techcrunch.com/2021/12/13/nike-acquires-nft-collectibles-studio-rtfkt/
[35] https://news.nike.com/news/nike-acquires-rtfkt
[36] www.linkedin.com/in/rogerbeaman/
[37] https://finance.yahoo.com/news/introducing-novel-no-code-platform-130000786.html#:~:text=The%20Novel%20founding%20team%20includes,and%20Founder%20of%20Sugar%20Capital

His experiences at Shutterstock and Goldman Sachs turned out to be quite helpful. "They mapped to the NFT/Web3 world more directly than you might think," said Beaman. "At Shutterstock, I worked on an in-browser image editor and pushed what was possible for in-browser experiences, which fed directly into the advanced tools we have to help creatives make NFTs with Novel. At Goldman, I worked on architecting a marketplace for complex financial products, and it was thinking this way that helped me map the market for NFTs and the role it made sense for Novel to play in it."[38]

The inspiration for Novel came when Beaman and his cofounders – Brian Sugar and Anna Merzi – began to see the impact of escalating ad acquisition costs for ecommerce. "We asked ourselves, is there a more sustainable, community-driven way to build a brand?" he said. "That's where NFTs fit into the marketer's playbook. Many brands have a latent community waiting to be activated. Web3 brings a brand closer to its customers and brings those customers closer to each other."

There was a problem, though. Many of the brands simply did not have the technical know-how for creating and managing NFTs. Thus, Beaman set forth to leverage no-code.

This means using easy-to-fill-out forms and drag-and-drop operations. There are no technical skills required or a deep background with cryptocurrencies and blockchain systems.

Here's how Novel works:

- Step 1 – Creation: The Novel Generator creates the artwork, sets the rarity, and establishes the royalty rates. The system then generates the underlying code for the smart contract.

- Step 2 – Sell: With the press of a few buttons, you can place your NFTs on the Shopify platform. Then customers can make purchases with a debit or credit card. There is no need for a crypto wallet.

- Step 3 – Minting: After the purchase, there is the creation for the token mint. Novel also covers all the gas fees for customers.

"We were inspired to create a platform that could democratize the relation-building components of Web3 by removing many barriers to entry, such as the need to understand crypto and blockchain technology," said Beaman.

---

[38] From the author's interview with Roger Beaman on May 12, 2022.

Novel is not just a technology either. The company also provides assistance with strategy. This is certainly very important given that many brands still lack much of an understanding of NFTs.

The pricing is based on a $99 monthly subscription for the software. Novel then takes a 10% fee for NFT sales and 1% to 2% for transactions on secondary marketplaces.[39]

As for Beaman's advice for entrepreneurs: "There is a ton of noise in the space and it's easy to get lost in that. To successfully build in the space, you need to cut through that and find your own truth. That's true in business generally, but it's especially true here. The keen insights at the heart of your business will likely sound pretty different from the present hype and media coverage of the space."

Fractal

Justin Kan is a pioneer of Internet video. While in his early 20s in 2007, he used a webcam – which was attached to his head – to broadcast his life, which he hosted on Justin.tv. This ignited the trend of "lifecasting."[40]

Kan did this for about eight months. And yes, it resulted in lots of publicity, which helped boost the traffic to Justin.tv.

Yet Kan saw there was a big business opportunity with this. He helped turn Justin.tv into a hub for video. He would then go on to help found Twitch. It helped to start another big trend – that is, the live streaming of video game play. This would ultimately lead to the birth of the eSports industry. Then in 2014, Twitch sold to Amazon for $970 million.[41] At the time, the platform had over 55 million users.

Keep in mind that Kan is not done with trying to find the next-big business. And he believes it has to do with NFTs. To this end, he cofounded Fractal in 2021. It's a marketplace for users to buy NFTs directly from game companies and is based on the Solana blockchain. Kan has raised $35 million for the venture.[42]

A key part of Fractal is Launchpad. This is a service that helps game companies sell their NFT collections.

---

[39] www.wsj.com/articles/novel-which-creates-nfts-for-companies-raises-6-million-11649154601?mod=lead_feature_below_a_pos1

[40] www.linkedin.com/in/justinkan/

[41] www.businessinsider.com/twitch-ceo-heres-why-we-sold-to-amazon-for-970-million-2014-8

[42] www.prnewswire.com/news-releases/twitch-co-founder-raises-35m-seed-round-for-fractal-a-new-marketplace-for-gaming-nfts-from-paradigm-and-multicoin-capital-301515486.html

But not just anyone can sell on the Fractal marketplace. There is extensive vetting, which helps to promote more quality and security (the company accepts only about 5% of submissions). Kan believes that the future of NFTs will require curation.

Some of the games on Fractal include Yaku (racing), House (real-time strategy), and Tiny Colony (a multi-mode game). All games on the marketplace have sold out their NFT collections.

Magic Eden

In 2021, Sidney Zhang, Jack Lu, Zhuoxun Yin, and Zhuojie Zhou cofounded Magic Eden. They all had deep roots in the tech world, with stints at companies like Uber Eats, Facebook AI, FTX, and Coinbase. A big attraction for the venture was the Solana blockchain. When Lu was at FTX, he had firsthand experience with this technology.

Magic Eden is a Web3-first marketplace for NFTs (Lu coined the name for the company because it is about the sense of limitless possibility). It was the first to allow bidding, a rarity index and a minting system that connects to a secondary marketplace. It has also quickly become the largest Solana-based platform. Here are some of the metrics:[43]

- 10+ million unique monthly visitors
- 4,000+ collections
- 100,000+ wallet connections
- $1 billion in secondary trading volume

The company has raised $27 million in venture capital.

OpenSea

Software engineer Devin Finzer cofounded Claimdog in 2015. It was a service that could find if a business owed you money. A year later, he would sell the company to Credit Karma. While there, Finzer learned about blockchain technology and saw it as fertile ground for his next startup.

His idea was WifiCoin. It allowed for the use of tokens to share wireless routers. Finzer got backing for this venture from Y Combinator. However, in a few months, he pivoted the business. Because of the popularity of CryptoKitties, he saw there was a bigger opportunity to create a marketplace for NFTs. So was born OpenSea.

---

[43] https://magiceden.io/about

While the company would grow, it was not until 2021 that there was an inflection point. As a result, Finzer had little difficulties raising substantial amounts of money from elite venture capital firms. By early 2022, he raised $300 million at a whopping $13.3 billion valuation.[44] The lead investors included Paradigm and Coatue Management.

With such strong backing, OpenSea has been able to recruit top-notch talent. The company was able to hire Brian Roberts, the former chief financial officer at Lyft, and Shiva Rajaraman, the previous vice president of commerce for Meta.

At the time of the funding, OpenSea generated over $2.4 billion in transaction volume for the month. This was up over 600X on a year-over-year basis.[45]

According to a blog post from Finzer: "We're focused on lowering the barriers to entry for NFTs by introducing features and simplified flows that abstract away the complexity of the blockchain. We're also accelerating our multi-chain support and prioritizing improvements to help people discover, manage, and showcase their NFTs with better tools, analytics, and presentation."[46]

Rarible

Alex Salnikov received a bachelor's degree in computer science and a master's degree in data science. This was a good background for his career in crypto. He went on to start various companies in the space. One he was able to sell.

His latest venture is Rarible, where he serves as the head of product. He also operates as a nomad. That is, he does not have a permanent residence. Instead, he lives primarily in Airbnbs in various parts of the world.

He cofounded Rarible in the summer of 2019. "We kept running into three types of people," he said. "One thought that crypto was too complex. The other believed there was no need for the technology and that they just needed a credit and debit card. Then there were those who were the diehard believers."[47]

For Alex, he saw an opportunity. He thought the timing was right to build a crypto marketplace for those who considered the technology too difficult.

At the time, the wallets were getting easier. "But there was not a lot of fun you could have with crypto," Alex said. "This is why we focused on NFTs."

---

[44] www.nytimes.com/2022/01/04/business/opensea-13-billion-valuation-venture-funding.html
[45] https://techcrunch.com/2022/01/04/nft-kingpin-opensea-lands-13-3b-valuation-in-300m-raise-from-paradigm-and-coatue/
[46] https://opensea.io/blog/announcements/announcing-openseas-new-funding/
[47] This was from the author's interview with Alex Salnikov on May 4, 2022.

His team was able to build a platform that made it easy for users to create and sell NFTs. "It just took a couple clicks for users," said Alex.

There was also the creation of an API. This made it possible for anyone to create their own Web3 marketplace.

The target market was crypto art. To build a following, Alex and his team bootstrapped the user base, such as by reaching out to communities on Twitter.

The strategy worked and Rarible started to grow. Yet the market would quickly shift. Users were becoming more interested in profile NFTs. "We had to change the direction of the company," said Alex. "But this is an advantage of a startup."

In building a successful Web3 firm, he believes that the founding team needs to be crypto native. This means that they must have a deep understanding of the technology, such as by reading the key whitepapers. If the interest about Web3 is mostly about being part of the next-big thing, then he thinks this will not work. "You need to believe in the core principles of Web3, like decentralization," said Alex. "This must be a part of your DNA."

In 2021, Rarible announced its Series A round. The company raised $14.2 million from Venrock Capital, CoinFund, and 01 Advisors.[48] At the time, the company had reached $150 million in sales.

Pastel Network

Anthony Georgiades and Jeff Emmanuel cofounded Pastel Network in 2018. They believed that the NFT market was poised to take off. However, they saw inherent problems. The NFT platforms were reliant primarily on existing Layer1 blockchains that were not built for the particular needs of NFTs.

With the Pastel Network, the founders created an application-specific Layer-1 blockchain. It reduced the high transaction fees, improved the security and lowered the inefficiencies. There were also features added to provide for counterfeit protection, authenticity, and permanent storage.

"From digital collectibles to media to documents to applications, users and developers are able to certify asset rareness and truly store data forever," said Georgiades. "Lightweight protocols delivered by interoperable open APIs such as Sense and Cascade can be easily integrated across existing networks.

---

[48] https://techcrunch.com/2021/06/23/nft-marketplace-startup-rarible-closes-14-2-million-series-a/

A wide range of Web3 applications can be built directly on the Pastel Network, enabling developers to enjoy the scalable registration features, storage processes, and security of the broader ecosystem."[49]

In terms of the security infrastructure, it is a multilayer technology protocol for the consensus mechanism. All network nodes use Proof-of-Work (PoW) while Pastel's decentralized network of SuperNodes currently use an innovative form of Proof-of-Stake (PoS).

The business model involves a modest transaction fee. There is a small amount that is burnt. This means it is taken out of the supply to serve as a way to avoid inflation of the tokens.

There are no licensing fees for integration partners. This has been critical in spreading the technology.

Regarding advice for Web3 entrepreneurs, Georgiades says: "First and foremost, entrepreneurs need to come into the space with a long-term outlook and objective. Technology, product development, and user adoption can take years to pan out. It is easy to get caught up in short-term excitement. However, it is important to stay prudent and patient when building new technologies and companies. With that in mind, entrepreneurs should really develop a good understanding of the basics - such as what is a blockchain or private key, how smart contracts work, and what does Web3 really entail? From there, you can start to gain a better knowledge of the various players in the ecosystem, where they all fit into the larger picture of Web3, and where innovation can be maximized."

He also believes that entrepreneurs need to make security a high priority. And this must start from day one. "Web3 isn't an inherently dangerous or risky space, but it is still in its early days and malicious users are taking advantage of that to scam and hack projects and consumers," said Georgiades. "One of the biggest ways to maximize security is prioritizing infrastructure and decentralization. A majority of failures come from overly centralized networks, managed by a small group of stakeholders, which are more susceptible to attacks. To avoid central points of failure, it's important to adequately distribute participants involved in reaching consensus and performing network operations. Nodes should also be distributed across a diverse range of users and entities, again, to avoid a single entity holding too many nodes, and thus too much control."

---

[49] From the author's interview with Anthony Georgiades on May 11, 2022.

Rally

Rob Petrozzo says that he cofounded Rally because of missed opportunities. For him, it was about being a fan of basketball superstar, Michael Jordan.

While as a teenager, he knew which sneakers he wore in specific games, which cars he drove to the arena, and just about every stat. "Even at a young age, I could have told you something as obvious as 'Michael Jordan's rookie card is going to be worth 6 figures one day,'" he said.[50]

But for Petrozzo, he did not have the access to collectibles or the resources to make a purchase.

So this is where Rally comes in. Launched in 2016, it is a fast-growing marketplace where you can buy and sell equity shares in ultra-rare assets, including NFTs. It's similar to how you would use an app like Robinhood to buy stocks. "At Rally, we wanted to solve that for every person who can see around the corners and would sooner invest in these items that they truly care about and obsess about, but don't know where to start," said Petrozzo. "To be able to turn that nostalgia or turn those aspirations into equity, and to allow people to do it at whatever price they're comfortable with is fulfilling that promise to the 10 year old me that said 'I'm going to have that one day.'"

Before starting the company, he had a successful career as a digital designer. He worked with clients across industries like music, publishing, and biotechnology. This experience was crucial in creating an engaging marketplace.

True, OpenSea is the clear dominant player in secondary transactions for NFTs. But Petrozzo realized there were other attractive categories to target.

"We've been able to give access to the most expensive and most recognized NFTs without having to onboard investors into an entirely new and often intimidating payment process," he said. "That's allowed us to take projects like Bored Ape Yacht Club and CryptoPunks, and run IPOs at around $10 per share, often putting more investors in single NFTs than there are total owners of all the NFTs in that particular project. Our first CryptoPunk NFT Initial Offering sold out incredibly quickly, and was purchased by nearly 4,000 unique investors. At that point, there were only around 3,800 total unique owners of all 10,000 CryptoPunks."

His advice to Web3 entrepreneurs is simple. Interestingly enough, it's similar to the iconic Nike motto: Just start the business.

---

[50] This is from the author's interview with Rob Petrozzo on May 5, 2022.

"The Web3 space is the true embodiment of creating a minimum viable product and building within the community as it grows," said Petrozzo. "Perfection is the enemy, and the stories around many of the biggest projects are still being written. If you can find a way to bring anything unique to the masses or build for an underserved audience, there's never been more access to the frameworks available in Web3. Build, release, and iterate based on the feedback of the community you're serving."

In late 2021, Rally announced a funding round of $15 million.[51] The lead investor was Wheelhouse. In all, the company has raised over $65 million.

Conclusion

In this chapter, we covered the various approaches to consumer Web3 applications. First, we looked at NFTs. They are a way to represent ownership in digital assets.

A key benefit is that the creator of NFTs can get a higher percentage of the revenues. It can also allow for building stronger connections with users.

But the values of NFTs are often subjective and volatile. There are also risks with hacking and fraud. Although, companies are investing in ways to mitigate these problems.

Despite all this, NFTs are likely to continue to be popular. The good news is that there has been more progress to deal with the problems.

NFTs are also likely to be the key for the emergence of Web3-style social networks and gaming platforms. They will be a visually interesting way to own digital items and make transactions. They will also allow users to move NFTs to other platforms, which should provide more value.

For Web3 games, they have been one of the early success stories. But then again, the industry has been a leader in transacting in digital items and deploying innovative business models. Web3 gaming is also likely to be the gateway for new users to participate in crypto.

Brands are also looking at NFTs and Web3 to connect with their customers. This can be an effective way to deal with the issues of privacy regulations.

In the next chapter, we'll take a look at DeFi or decentralized finance.

---

[51] https://news.yahoo.com/rally-secures-15-million-latest-160045886.html

DeFi

Building Finance Platforms

Kwon Do, who studied computer science at Stanford, has worked at companies like Apple and Microsoft. But when crypto started to grow quickly, he jumped into the market. Unfortunately, his first startup failed. But this did not deter him. In 2018, he started another company, called Terraform Labs, based in Singapore.

His vision was to create a new kind of financial services company. It was based on a Web3 approach called DeFi or decentralized finance. To this end, he created several projects and apps, such as for payments. At the heart of this was the LUNA token. By 2021, its value would reach $41 billion.[1]

Kwon also created UST, which was an algorithmic stable coin. It was set to have a 1:1 peg to the US dollar. However, UST was only backed by complex equations, not other financial assets.

By early May, LUNA would crumble. Within a week, it would drop to nearly zero.[2]

---

[1] https://finance.yahoo.com/news/kwon-humbled-luna-spirals-ust-16101 1471.html

[2] www.fa-mag.com/news/cryptocurrencies-crater-as-terra-collapse-trig-gers-defi-exodus-67829.html

© Tom Taulli 2022
T. Taulli, *How to Create a Web3 Startup*,
https://doi.org/10.1007/978-1-4842-8683-8_7

What happened? There were a variety of factors at work. The equities markets were plunging as well as many other cryptocurrencies. There were also fears of a recession and tighter Federal Reserve policies.

Ultimately, for LUNA, it was a classic case of a "run on the bank." Simply put, investors lost trust in this digital asset. But there was no government backing. So there could not be any bailout.

Yes, this showed the inherent risks of DeFi. The result is that the future is far from secure.

But this an important wake-up call that can lead to better protections. If anything, it could allow for a much more robust industry.

So, in this chapter, we'll take a look at DeFi. If it can get critical mass, there is the potential for it to become a huge market for entrepreneurs.

What Is DeFi?

Like most parts of Web3, DeFi is fairly new. The origins go back to 2018.[3] It was during a chat on Telegram, in which developers and founders were trying to come up with a good way to describe blockchain-based financial systems.

The traditional financial market – which is referred to as TradeFi – is mostly centralized. There are various institutions like banks, investment banks, and brokerages that handle trades. The industry also has extensive regulations.

With DeFi, the goal is to breakdown these barriers and allow peer-to-peer transactions. This is likely to lead to lower costs, less paperwork, and faster settlements.

In a sense, DeFi is about disrupting the main parts of TradeFi. They include lending, savings, insurance, derivatives, just to name a few. For the most part, DeFi systems are based on Ethereum smart contracts. By contrast, TradeFi generally has a legacy technology infrastructure. It's common for systems to be based on mainframe computers and legacy languages like COBOL.

Some of the other benefits of DeFi include:

- Democratization of Financial Services: According to research from the World Bank, about 1.7 billion people across the globe do not have a bank account.[4] This is certainly a huge problem as it can mean huge challenges

---

[3] https://qz.com/2065446/everything-you-need-to-know-about-decentralized-finance-defi/
[4] www.yahoo.com/video/world-bank-1-7-billion-152239354.html

for dealing with poverty. But with DeFi, it is possible to provide wider access to financial services. All that is needed is a basic smartphone and access to the Internet.

- Income: DeFi can provide higher yields on investments. True, this means taking on more risks. But this may be worth it for certain people. DeFi also can be a way to diversify a portfolio of traditional investments.

- Settlement: With a transaction using a check, the processing takes three days. But DeFi has near instantaneous settlement.

- Tokenization: The use of tokens can allow for ownership of larger assets, such as artwork, a business, or real estate. This can help raise capital for projects. It can also mean that more people will have access to investments that usually have been available to wealthy people and investments funds.

- Availability: Wall Street is open from 9:30 am to 4:00 pm on weekdays. A bank may have similar hours. However, with DeFi, the transactions can happen on a 24/7 basis.

Note   According to DeFi Pulse, the total value of the market for DeFi is about $56 billion.[5]

DeFi has been primarily focused on B2C (business-to-consumer) applications. But this is starting to change. The B2B (business-to-business) category is picking up momentum. In fact, the opportunities could be larger. B2B DeFi has the potential to allow for a more efficient financial infrastructure. In fact, mega operators like Visa, MasterCard, and various banks have been investing in this.

dApp Process for DeFi

Along with other crypto apps, DeFi can be somewhat cumbersome. It's true that there continues to be progress. Since DeFi is still in the early-adopter phase, there continues to be much room for improvement with the UI and UX.

Perhaps the biggest issue is that there are multiple steps, and you usually need to access multiple products.

---

[5] www.defipulse.com/

So then, let's take a look at a typical workflow (this assumes you already understand how to use a crypto wallet) for staking. Staking is a way to lock and hold your asset for a longer time frame under a smart contract. It means that you can gain benefits like rewards, voting power, and interest.

Here are the steps:

- You will connect your crypto wallet to the website or mobile app. At this stage, you want to be cautious. Is this an illegitimate URL or mobile app? You might want to do a Google search on this.

- The dApp will require you to sign a transaction.

- The dApp will authorize your access. Once this is complete, you can do a stake.

- You will make a transaction and confirm it. It will be included on the particular blockchain. Although, there may be other pending transactions. After this, you will be staked.

DeFi Ecosystem

Even though DeFi is relatively new, there has been an explosion of innovation. Here are just some of the interesting applications available:

- Decentralized exchanges (DEXs): This is a marketplace for trading US dollars and other fiat currencies for cryptocurrencies. There are also services like Uniswap, which allow for trades that have lower fees.

- Lending and borrowing: With DeFi, you can lend money to anyone around the globe. Or you can deposit your crypto to earn interest or get rewards. The interest rates can be at double-digit levels. A leader in DeFi borrowing and lending services is AAVE, which is based on the Ethereum blockchain.

- Mortgages: Some DeFi startups, like Figure, allow their users to borrow against their crypto to make home purchases. This is based on the provenance blockchain. Some startups, such as LoanSnap, can transform your mortgage into an NFT, which allows for much faster processing.

- Yield Farming: This is a service – based on a DEX – that searches for higher returns from various tokens. This can be a very high-risk activity, though.

- Prediction markets: This is where you can place a wager on a certain future event, such as the election of the President.

Risks

When it comes to the risks of DeFi, it is similar to any type of financial service. It's about the potential of losing your money. For example, it could be from a scam or a hack.

But there are also technology risks. Faulty coding of a smart contract can also be a big problem. There are cases where this has resulted in millions in lost funds.

Even highly sophisticated investors have suffered major losses. Just look at Internet entrepreneur and investor, Mark Cuban. He invested in a DeFi token that plunged to zero in one day! He tweeted: "I got hit like everyone else. Crazy part is I got out, thought they were increasing their TVL enough. Than Bam."[6]

According to research from CipherTrace, the losses from DeFi fraud has been rising. During the first quarter of 2022, they came to $156 million.[7]

Yet DeFi remains a small market. It is geared really to early adopters and crypto believers. But if DeFi continues to grow quickly, this could pose a risk to the economy. It could be similar to what happened during the financial crisis, in which there was a massive breakdown of the mortgage market. A big part of this was due to highly complex financial derivatives.

Note that its common for a DeFi application to have the user put up collateral. This is to provide more support to the financial system. However, the collateral is usually in cryptocurrencies, which can be volatile. In other words, this can ultimately lead to major losses. In some cases, the DeFi application may liquidate positions.

To mitigate this problem, a DeFi system can have a stable coin as the token. But this is far from foolproof too.

Note   An impermanent loss is a temporary loss for a DeFi system. This often happens because of imbalances with supply-and-demand in the marketplace. For this, the DeFi platform will transfer a return to the token holders. This usually is enough. But this approach is no guarantee. Unfortunately, there are DeFi systems that ultimately fail.

---

[6]www.benzinga.com/markets/cryptocurrency/21/06/21611813/mark-cuban-got-hit-like-everyone-else-as-defi-token-crashed-from-65-to-0
[7]www.cnbc.com/2021/06/18/whats-defi-crypto-based-decentralized-finance-explained.html

Disruption

No doubt, a common goal for entrepreneurs is disruption. When successful, the returns can be substantial.

As for DeFi, the market opportunity is actually one of the biggest. For example, according to PayPal CEO Dan Schulman, the estimated size for digital payments is $100 trillion.[8]

Yet this is just one segment of the industry. There are other massive markets like insurance, investments, and lending.

In light of this, there should be no surprise that there are many DeFi players that are gunning for the market opportunities. And this is not necessarily something for entrepreneurs to worry about. It's a validation of the category. Besides, there should be room for a variety of firms to become strong players.

If anything, one of the worst things an entrepreneur can say is that there is "no or little competition." For most investors, this is a red flag.

Even though the market opportunity is massive for DeFi, this does not mean that this approach to finance will ultimately win out.

The fact is that traditional financial institutions are not sitting back. They understand the importance of innovation.

Here's what JPMorgan Chase CEO Jamie Dimon wrote in his 2021 shareholder letter: "Decentralized finance and blockchain are real, new technologies that can be deployed in both public and private fashion, permissioned or not. JPMorgan Chase is at the forefront of this innovation. We use a blockchain network called Link to enable banks to share complex information, and we also use a blockchain to move tokenized US dollar deposits with JPM Coin. We believe there are many uses where a blockchain can replace or improve contracts, data ownership and other enhancements; for some purposes, however, it is currently too expensive or too slow to be deployed."[9]

But for a DeFi startup, an effective strategy may be to partner with traditional financial institutions. This allows for leveraging existing distribution channels and strong brands. As for the DeFi startup, it can focus on the technology development.

---

[8] www.itbusinessedge.com/networking/decentralized-finance/
[9] https://reports.jpmorganchase.com/investor-relations/2021/ar-ceo-letters.htm

Total Value Locked (TVL)

A key metric for DeFi is total value locked or TVL. This shows the total amount of assets for a protocol or network.

While this does provide a good sense of the success, TVL is far from perfect. Let's face it, the value may suddenly fall or even collapse. It's not uncommon for users of a project to move to another one. Maintaining a Web3 community is no easy feat.

So, it is important to look at other metrics. Some of them include the following:

- Engagement of the community.

- Integrations of the protocol with other applications, exchanges, and wallets.

- A growing number of token holders. This may indicate positive word-of-mouth marketing.

- Increases in the number of developers.

OK then, as for the rest of the chapter, we'll take a look at some of the interesting startups in the DeFi space.

Tribal

Amr Shady and Mohamed Elkasstawi are top entrepreneurs in Egypt. But they experienced firsthand the challenges of running businesses in the Middle East – especially in terms of getting financing. The paperwork and regulations are usually expensive and time-consuming. The criteria for funding is often too onerous for smaller businesses.

But Shady and Elkasstawi saw an opportunity to leverage blockchain to create a new type of platform.[10] The company, Tribal, was launched in late 2019.

Tribal's system, which includes a business credit card, uses a sophisticated AI approval process.[11] This has greatly streamlined the process. Tribal has also a variety of services like local and international wires and spend management. There are customers in 22 countries.

---

[10] www.menabytes.com/tribal-credit-seed/#:~:text=Tribal%20Credit%2C%20 a%20San%20Francisco%2Dbased%20fintech%20startup%20co%2D,in%20a%20state-ment%20to%20MENAbytes
[11] www.tribal.credit/who-we-are

In early 2022, the company raised $60 million in a Series B round.[12] The investors included the SoftBank Latin America Fund, BECO Capital, QED Investors, and Rising Tide. The total funding has come to over $140 million.

According to Shu Nyatta, Managing Partner of SoftBank Latin America Fund: "Tribal is using crypto to fundamentally change the rules of the game for payments and lending. Very few companies can bridge TradeFi and DeFi in such an innovative, yet seamless way."[13]

Valora

In the early 2000s, Jackie Bona graduated from UCLA with a B.A. in international relations and history. Yet she would quickly become a successful marketing pro.[14] She spent over seven years at Google and then went on to Twitter and Spotify. At these companies, she learned about how to hack growth and develop easy-to-use applications. During her stints, she lived in nine countries that spanned four continents.

By 2021, Bona became a tech founder. She launched Valora, which focused on a mobile-first crypto wallet for borderless payments. She is the CEO and has raised about $20 million.

The app is for newbies as well as experienced crypto traders. It's available in over 100 countries and the fees are low, at a mere $0.001. Yes, it is nearly free to use. This has not only helped gin up adoption but has also made it practical in developing nations where the transaction amounts are usually small.

The simplicity of the app is another critical feature. You do not have to use 42-character wallet addresses. Instead, you just need a phone number to send money.

Valora has a lucrative rewards system, which is at 25% of the balance. This helps to encourage more transactions.

Valero uses the Celo blockchain, which has its origins with Ethereum. However, they are both independent of each other. This means that Celo wallets cannot connect with the Ethereum network.

Celo is focused on stablecoins, such as those based on the US dollar, the riyal, and the euro. Next, there is full support for ERC-20 tokens. This allows for the porting over of dApps. For example, here are some that Valora offers:

---

[12] www.tribal.credit/press-releases/tribal-raises-60m-in-oversubscribed-series-b-led-by-softbank-latin-america-fund

[13] www.tribal.credit/press-releases/tribal-raises-60m-in-oversubscribed-series-b-led-by-softbank-latin-america-fund

[14] www.linkedin.com/in/jackiebona/

- Celo Tracker: This manages your portfolio for NFTs and other digital assets.

- Bidali: This uses gift cards for popular brands.

- ChiSpend – Super App: You can use cryptocurrencies to buy real-world products and services.

- Celo Tax: This provides tax analysis of your transactions.

Celo is also environmentally friendly. Note that it has a carbon-negative infrastructure.

TrustToken

Rafael Cosman has worked as a machine-learning engineer at companies like Palantir, Kernel, and Google. But he saw crypto as a massive opportunity and founded TrustToken in 2017.[15] He wanted to create a next-generation financial services company. Cosman has raised about $34 million for his startup.

There are two main parts to TrustToken. There is TrueFX, which is a set of stablecoins for the US dollar, British pound sterling, the Canadian dollar, and so on. Next, there is TrueFi, which is a DeFi platform that is built on the Ethereum blockchain. The focus is primarily on providing uncollateralized loans.

Keep in mind that this is fairly unique. The reason is that crypto lending is generally over-collateralized. While this allows for more safety, it does limit the potential for the market. Note that the opportunity is massive. Traditional unsecured lending is about $11 trillion on a global basis.[16]

TrustToken's loans also have the advantage of providing lenders higher returns. But there needs to be ways to provide standards for credit scoring. This is similar to the FICO score for traditional lending.

Here's how it works: TrustToken provides a system for lenders to easily store their money. Then the borrows send credit requests. The interest and limits are based on the borrower's credit score. But the community must vote on each loan. Essentially, this is a reputation-based way for allocating loans. Although, if the borrower does not repay the loan, there will be potential legal consequences.

As of early 2022, TrustToken has processed over $524 million in loans and paid more than $17.5 million in interest.[17]

---

[15] www.linkedin.com/in/rafaelcosman/details/experience/
[16] https://techstory.in/truefi-everything-you-need-to-know-about-it/
[17] https://truefi.io/

0x Labs

0x Labs is one of the first DeFi protocols and the operator of Matcha, which is a crypto exchange. According to CEO and cofounder, Amir Bandeali: "When we were starting 0x almost six years ago, we had this thesis that everything of value would eventually be tokenized."[18]

The core business of 0x Labs is integration services. With these, companies are able to create their own Web3 platforms, such as allowing for using tokens. For example, the technology powers the NFT marketplace for Coinbase.

0x Labs supports seven large blockchains, which include Ethereum, Polygon, Fantom, Avalanche, Optimism, BNB Chain, and Celo. There are also integrations with the top wallets and apps like MetaMask, Coinbase Wallet, Polygon Wallet, Brave, Matcha, dYdX, Zapper, Zerion, and Shapeshift. 0x Labs has tokenized over $157 billion in value.[19]

In April 2022, the company raised $70 million. In a blog post from one of the investors – Greylock – had this to say: "At Greylock, we especially love to back companies that arm the builders: developers and entrepreneurs. 0x Labs is one of these companies. While some may believe that decentralization of exchange is infeasible and users will gravitate to a small handful of already-leading exchanges and wallets, we take the opposite view. We believe we're at the very early innings of re-building our financial infrastructure on new rails, where the minimum future trading volume encapsulates all existing traditional financial assets, and the expected end state includes an ownership economy across social networks, games, other real-world assets, and more."[20]

Conclusion

DeFi remains relatively small, but there is enormous potential for entrepreneurs. The technology allows for much more streamlined, faster, and cheaper financial transactions. DeFi can also greatly expand access to financial services, especially in developing countries.

---

[18] https://finance.yahoo.com/news/ox-labs-bandeali-says-everything-072114118.html
[19] www.businesswire.com/news/home/20220426006160/en/0x-Labs-Raises-70M-Led-By-Greylock-to-Continue-Expanding-Web3%E2%80%99s-Core-Exchange-Infrastructure
[20] https://greylock.com/portfolio-news/exchange-infrastructure-for-the-internet/

But there are certainly risks. With little regulation, there have already been problems with breaches and malfunctions. Yet this means entrepreneurs can build systems for better security and stability.

The opportunities are not just for B2C applications. The B2B space could actually be a bigger market. Some of the world's largest financial services companies have been investing in DeFi.

As for the next chapter, we'll take a look at the metaverse.

The Metaverse

Startups in the Virtual World

Facebook's Mark Zuckerberg has a knack for making great strategic decisions. Just some include the acquisition of Instagram and the pivot to mobile.

But his next move will certainly be the biggest. It's about the metaverse. This is essentially a virtual world, which involves life-like immersive experiences.

In October 2021, Zuckerberg announced his bold plans. He renamed the company to Meta. This was largely due to Zuckerberg's interest in Greek literature and history, which he studied at Harvard. The word "meta" means "beyond" in Greek.

Zuckerberg said the plan was to spend over $10 billion on the metaverse – and this could grow over the coming years.[1] Keep in mind that he has already made other important investments in the category, such as with the acquisition of Oculus, which is a top developer of VR (Virtual Reality) gear and software.

But the realization of the metaverse will not be immediate. There is still much to be done. According to Zuckerberg: "Building the foundational platforms for the metaverse will be a long road. Later in this decade is when we would sort of expect this to be more of a real business story."[2]

---

[1] www.wsj.com/articles/mark-zuckerberg-to-sketch-out-facebooks-metaverse-vision-11635413402
[2] www.wsj.com/articles/mark-zuckerberg-to-sketch-out-facebooks-metaverse-vision-11635413402

© Tom Taulli 2022
T. Taulli, *How to Create a Web3 Startup*,
https://doi.org/10.1007/978-1-4842-8683-8_8

This will certainly mean lots of opportunities for entrepreneurs. Note that Facebook has been aggressive with acquisitions in the space.

The metaverse will also be a key part of Web3. It will rely on the capabilities of crypto to allow for transactions as well as a decentralized model.

In this chapter, we'll take a deeper look at the metaverse and get a sense of the different places where entrepreneurs can participate.

■ **Note**   Zuckerberg's aggressive move to the metaverse has many skeptics. Some believe that this is mostly about PR, so as to avoid the negative aspects of social media. Others say that Zuckerberg is being defensive and is trying to find ways to attract a younger demographic. Regardless, he has huge amounts of resources to make a big impact on the market and to shape the industry. Already the metaverse has become one of the most talked about concepts in the tech world.

What Is the Metaverse?

Neal Stephenson, a top science fiction writer, coined the word "metaverse" in 1992. It was in the novel, Snow Crash.

Since then, the metaverse has become a popular theme for science fiction writers. Just look at the widely successful Ready Player One, by Ernest Cline. Steven Spielberg adapted this into a hit movie in 2018.

But as of now, the metaverse is becoming more than science fiction. There are already a variety of virtual environments that have gained traction.

A key to the metaverse is the avatar. This is your representation in the environment. You can make yourself look cool, hot, weird, dorky. You can also have different avatars – depending on the context.

Although, there are some drawbacks. Avatars currently only show a person from the waist up! Why is this so? The reason is that most people interact with the metaverse by wearing VR headsets. But there are no sensors for the legs.

Despite this, the metaverse provides lots of potential:

- Go on a virtual vacation to Paris, the moon, Mars, or even a planet in another galaxy.
- Shop at a store. It could be Harrod's in London.

- Learn about physics. Perhaps the professor could be Albert Einstein or Max Plank.

- Check out a baseball game. You can also be one of the batters.

- Meet singles. You could use crypto to buy a gift for someone you are wooing.

The money-making potential is also significant. Consider the analysis from Jefferies analyst Andrew Uerkwitz. He believes the metaverse could easily generate revenues over $80 billion.[3] The reason is that this is the amount already spent on virtual goods in video games.

The metaverse represents a generational leap in technology. It could be similar to the impact of the graphical user interface in the 1980s with the Macintosh; the Web in the 1990s; or the smartphone in the 2010s.

But the metaverse could be even more impactful. It will be a transition from the two-dimensional world of the computer screen to the 3D world. It will actually seem like you are in another world. For example, you will be able to feel it, such as through haptic systems.

In the metaverse, the interactions with other people will be more normal, more human. Here's how Zuckerberg describes it: "The defining quality of the metaverse will be a feeling of presence — like you are right there with another person or in another place. Feeling truly present with another person is the ultimate dream of social technology. That is why we are focused on building this."[4]

This is in stark contrast with traditional online and social media platforms. It's more like interacting in a flat world, where communication is based on texts, emails, likes, posts, and videos.

Note Dating app Tinder is investing heavily in building its own metaverse. To this end, it has made several acquisitions, such as to add real-time video. The company has also introduced its own crypto token: Tinder Coin.[5] Members will be able to use these for features like Boost and Super Like as well as to encourage profile verifications and creating video intros.

---

[3] www.wsj.com/articles/mark-zuckerberg-sets-facebook-on-long-costly-path-to-metaverse-reality-11635252726
[4] https://about.fb.com/news/2021/10/founders-letter/
[5] https://techcrunch.com/2021/11/03/match-group-details-plans-for-a-dating-metaverse-tinders-virtual-goods-based-economy/

Interestingly enough, one of the biggest growth areas for the metaverse is virtual land speculation. Some of the purchases are in the millions.[6] There are even investment firms that are focused on this opportunity, like Tokens.com.

Large Tech Firms and the Metaverse

Meta is not the only megatech company that is investing enormous amounts in the metaverse. All the major operators are focused on this, including Google, Microsoft, and Apple.

Let's take a look at Microsoft. The company certainly has many advantages with the metaverse. It has huge cash resources, a large base of talented employees, a strong global infrastructure, and a massive number of customers. Then there is its Xbox franchise. This will definitely be a solid foundation for creating a metaverse.

But Microsoft has ambitious plans to build on this. In early 2022, the company announced the $70 billion acquisition of Activision Blizzard. It has nearly 400 million MAUs (Monthly Active Users) and franchises like Call of Duty, Diablo, Word of Warcraft, and Candy Crush.[7]

For the announcement of the deal, Microsoft CEO Satya Nadella said, "In gaming, we see the metaverse as a collection of communities and individual identities anchored in strong content franchises accessible on every device." He also said that the deal for Activision would be critical for creating Microsoft's own metaverse.[8]

But Nadella believes that there will not just be a few large ones. He, instead, believes that the world will have many of them. This is why a big priority for Microsoft is to be the go-to tools provider for the metaverse.

This technology will not be easy to create. It will need to use highly sophisticated hardware systems and graphics. There will also need to be a way to allow users to create their own environments.

Although, online games are a good place to start – and this sector is likely to dominate the emerging industry of the metaverse. Let's face it, many of the users spend hours playing games. They would also like to help with the world building and have the potential to benefit from the financial incentives.

---

[6] www.wsj.com/articles/the-metaverse-isnt-quite-ready-for-you-but-your-investment-is-welcome-11640779204
[7] https://investor.activision.com/static-files/180f309f-89e2-4fb8-a98d-b527edfdaf46
[8] www.polygon.com/22917625/microsoft-activision-blizzard-metaverse-satya-nadella

> ▓ **Note** Among the megatech operators, Apple has been mostly silent about its plans for the metaverse. But it seems like a good bet the company is focused on this opportunity. Keep in mind that it has invested heavily in AR (Augmented Reality).

Another benefit for the involvement of larger tech companies is the standardization. If not, there could be too much fragmentation in the metaverse. "A true metaverse will require seamless interoperability among users and platforms, based on still-to-be-determined standards," said George Korizis, who is the Customer Transformation Leader at PwC US.[9]

However, this is not to imply that the large tech companies will dominate the category. The market is likely to be massive. So, there should be lots of opportunities for smaller companies and startups.

Consider Snap. The company was an early adopter of AR. At first, the move was considered somewhat trivial. Snap allowed users to easily create avatars.

But it has turned out to be very popular. Snap says that users are using the AR technology more than six billion times a day.[10] This technology will prove useful with the metaverse.

Or look at Unity. Founded in 2004, the company is a leader in gaming development tools. The founders are David Helgason, Nicholas Francis, and Joachim Ante, who launched the company in the Netherlands. They initially created a game, but it failed. However, by doing this, the founders made some useful tools. So, they decided to focus on this opportunity.

And it was a great move. In 2021, revenues shot up by 44% to $1.1 billion.[11] Currently, the platform handles five billion downloads per month and has 3.9 billion users.[12] About 72% of the top mobile games use Unity.

At the heart of the company's technology is RT3D or real-time 3D technology. This allows for the creation of fully interactive 3D environments. The rendering is done in microseconds, which provides for a seamless experience.

---

[9] From the author's interview with George Korizis on April 20, 2022.
[10] www.wsj.com/articles/the-metaverse-isnt-quite-ready-for-you-but-your-investment-is-welcome-11640779204
[11] https://investors.unity.com/news/news-details/2022/Unity-Announces-Fourth-Quarter-and-Full-Year-2021-Financial-Results/default.aspx
[12] https://unity.com/our-company

"The metaverse only exists because of technologies like RT3D," said Peter Moore, who is the SVP and GM of Sports and Live Entertainment at Unity. "The ability to create, build, influence, or manipulate something that can transfer between physical and digital and back again can only be done by using this approach."[13]

The Challenges

When Zuckerberg said the metaverse will take a long time, he was being very realistic. This was probably not an attempt to downplay expectations.

First of all, the metaverse currently requires significant compute power. Consider the example of Decentraland. Founded in 2017, the company is one of the top metaverse platforms. With it, you can buy virtual plots of land using NFTs that are based on the MANA cryptocurrency.

But to play the game, you need a desktop computer that has a sophisticated GPU (Graphics Processing Unit) chip from Nvidia or Advanced Micro Devices. In other words, this will cost thousands of dollars more than a typical computer.

With the metaverse, you will also need a VR headset. True, the prices have come down on these devices. For example, Meta's Oculus can cost between $300 and $500.

Yet the issue with VR headsets is the experience. Earlier in this chapter, we have noted that there are usually no legs in the visuals of the metaverse. But there are other problems as well.

Perhaps the most notable one is that VR headsets can cause motion sickness. In some cases, people will throw up!

Another problem has to do with space. What if you walk down a long pathway? Well, this may not work too well since you may be in a small room.

There have also been cases where people have bumped into walls or other objects. Sometimes this has resulted in injuries – even broken bones.[14] There is even the "gorilla arm syndrome." This is pain that results from having your arms raised for a long period of time.

---

[13] From the author's interview with Peter Moore on April 9, 2022.
[14] www.wsj.com/articles/restaurants-virtual-stores-test-consumers-appetite-for-metaverse-marketing-11649160001

Regardless, there continues to be progress with VR headsets. They are getting easier to use and more powerful. The growth has also been strong. According to IDC, the shipments of VR headsets are expected to reach 28.7 million on a global basis by 2025.[15]

Besides the issues with the gear, there will need to be major upgrades to existing Internet infrastructure. It's true that 5G will be a big help with latency. But there will probably need to be substantial investments in data centers. The amount of data required for immersive experiences is enormous.

Another nagging issue with the metaverse is AI. To make this work, there will be a need for access to the right kinds of data, which allows the algorithms to learn over time. Then there are the difficulties with privacy and bias.

If the data is not managed properly, the experience could be strange indeed. The shapes and movements in the environment could be out-of-sync of what's expected.

Although, there are innovations to help out. AI is getting better at using synthetic data. As the name implies, this is artificial data that is based on certain extrapolations or assumptions. This can allow for much higher volumes of data that is fairly clean.

"We're entering a new era of data-centric AI development whereby tapping into the virtual world of real-time 3D we can make the world a better place with synthetic data," said Danny Lange, who is the SVP of AI at Unity. "Synthetic data is important because it's generated to meet specific needs or conditions that are not available in existing data. This can be useful in numerous cases, such as when privacy requirements limit data availability or dictate how it can be used. The benefits extend to overcoming unwanted bias in real-world data."[16]

Something else: It's not clear how much adoption there will be of the metaverse. For example, early incarnations like Second Life turned out to be niches. Then again, they did not have the extensive technologies that exist today. Yet it does seem like there will probably be a considerable number of people who would prefer not to participate. Hey, they may just prefer their own physical universe!

On the other hand, there will be other people who will want to spend all their time in the metaverse. It's actually similar to the problem parents have with children who constantly play video games.

---

[15] www.wsj.com/articles/big-tech-seeks-its-next-fortune-in-the-metaverse-11636459200
[16] From the author's interview with Danny Lange on April 18, 2022.

The bottom line: The metaverse has lots of unknowns. But this is not stopping entrepreneurs. The fact is that there will be continued focus on this category.

■ **Note** To deal with the special issues with the metaverse, entrepreneurs are looking at developing creative solutions. For example, one option is omnidirectional treadmills, which allow for simulating walking in a large area. In fact, some real estate developers are making homes that have their own metaverse rooms.[17]

Marketing in the Metaverse

While the focus for Web3 business models is on crypto payments, the business opportunity may be somewhat different with the metaverse. Granted, crypto will still be very important, since there will be a virtual economy. But branding is likely to be another crucial part of monetization.

The marketing impact is likely to be better than a typical banner ad or a video embedded in a Facebook feed. The advertising for the metaverse will become part of an immersive and engaging environment.

An interesting example is Roblox. The origins of the company go back to 1989. Founders David Baszucki and Erik Cassel developed a popular 2D software system to simulate a physics lab for students. Leveraging on this experience, they would then go on to create the Roblox platform in 2004. Although, this virtual world was 3D. It also had tools like the Roblox Studio to allow users to create their own items, games, and applications. They could then sell them.

Currently, the DAUs (daily active users) are close to 50 million.[18] In 2021, the company posted $1.9 billion in revenues, up 108% on a year-over-year basis.

Then what about the marketing opportunities for brands? Well, one interesting example is the Chipotle Burritor Builder.[19] This is a simulation on the Roblox platform. Basically, it's a contest to see who can successfully roll burritos, which can be tricky. For this, the winners earn Burrito Bucks. You can use these to buy entrees from the Chipotle app and Chipotle.com.

---

[17] www.wsj.com/articles/why-homes-of-the-future-will-have-spaces-for-the-metaverse-11649427017
[18] www.sec.gov/ix?doc=/Archives/edgar/data/0001315098/000131509822000058/rblx-20211231.htm
[19] https://newsroom.chipotle.com/2022-04-05-FANS-CAN-ROLL-BURRITOS-AT-CHIPOTLE-IN-THE-METAVERSE-TO-EARN-BURRITOS-IN-REAL-LIFE

Another example is Molson Coors Beverage. The beer maker teamed up with Decentralized to create a virtual bar.[20] Users could pour beer and talk with other people. There was even an option to play the jukebox. Molson Coors Beverage selected Decentralize because the platform is only viewed from the browser and allows for restricting users by age.

The average user spent about 20 minutes at the virtual bar. All in all, this marketing effort was likely more engaging than just a typical ad.

As should be no surprise, Meta is already experimenting with marketing opportunities with its own metaverse. This has certainly been the case with the Horizon platform, which is integrated with Oculus VR headsets. Users can explore thousands of different virtual worlds and even create their own.

In 2022, Wendy's launched its own on Horizon. The company called it the Wendyverse, which is a virtual restaurant.[21] The focus was for the March Madness college basketball tournament. The Wendyverse allowed users to shoot baskets and do slam dunks.

The Enterprise

Much of the activity for the metaverse has been with gaming and other consumer applications. But this is likely to change – and perhaps soon. Enterprises are also seeing the huge potential of this market.

"There is a major opportunity for the industrial metaverse," said Lange. "The goal is not about social interaction. Rather, it's about simulating experiences in the virtual world before moving into the physical world."

This could be bigger than the consumer opportunity. Just look at the global supply chain. Because of the impact of the Covid-19 pandemic, it has been under tremendous stress. The result has been scarcity of items and higher inflation.

But the metaverse could be a major help. Because of the 3D visuals, it can be easier to understand the workflows. This will mean that you can spot the bottlenecks and find more optimal approaches.

---

[20] www.wsj.com/articles/marketers-explore-metaverse-worlds-11646218800
[21] www.marketingdive.com/news/wendys-metaverse-meta-horizon-worlds/621325/

Here's a look at what some companies are doing with enterprise applications in the metaverse:

- In late 2021, Accenture ordered 60,000 Quest 2 virtual reality headsets.[22] The reason was for training and onboarding. The company was planning on hiring up to 125,000 new employees and VR could help streamline the process. But the use of the headsets could also be a way for the company's consultants to better understand the technology and find ways to help their clients. When it comes to enterprise systems, a big factor in getting adoption is the buy-in from IT consultants. For Accenture, this order was just the first phase in the company's aggressive VR roadmap.

- Nike has filed several trademarks for "Nike," "Just Do it," "Air Jordan," "Jumpman," and the swoosh logo.[23] The reason? The company appears to be making moves to sell digital items in the metaverse. Nike also has been hiring virtual material designers. According to one job ad: "You will have a deep understanding of shading models, material capture solutions, rendering technology, and can seamlessly navigate between real-time and path tracing platforms. You are passionate about designing new materials and developing the look of a scene to tell a story!"[24]

- BMW has partnered with Nvidia to use VR, robotics, and AI for smart factories.[25] This is done by using Nvidia's Enterprise Omniverse platform. There is also the use of the EGX edge computing system, the Aerial software development kits for high-end GPUs, and software-defined 5G wireless radio to access networks on the factory floor. With all this, design teams at BMW can collaborate in a 3D environment. The result is that a factory line can manufacture up to ten unique cars, with more than 100 options. The system also emulates digital

---

[22] www.xrtoday.com/virtual-reality/accenture-orders-record-60000-oculus-headsets/
[23] www.cnbc.com/2021/11/02/nike-is-quietly-preparing-for-the-meta-verse-.html
[24] https://jobs.nike.com/job/00578450
[25] https://blogs.nvidia.com/blog/2021/04/13/nvidia-bmw-factory-future/

humans, which are used to test new workflows in a simulation. This helps to speed up the development process and lower the costs

- The Johnson & Johnson Institute teamed up with Osso VR and Oculus for Business.[26] The goal was to improve training for surgeons. Keep in mind that a big part of training has been for residents to observe experienced surgeons. While this is certainly effective, it is difficult to scale. The problem is that surgeons need to know about many more complex systems and devices. To better deal with this, Johnson & Johnson was able to create a virtual environment for getting realistic simulations of using implant orthopedic devices. For example, when doing intramedullary nailing of a tibia, the scores for students were 233% higher compared to passive learning tools.

But metaverse technologies do not have to be this grand. After all, many companies do not have these sophisticated needs or the resources for these investments. Yet there are still many use cases for the metaverse for smaller organizations.

One area is with workplace communications. It's true that offerings like Zoom, Google Meet, and FaceTime have been effective. But there are still limitations.

"With the metaverse, we will move toward more seamless interactions between people all over the physical world," said Rebecca Binny, who is the Director of PR + Marketing for RayCo Media.[27] "Coming together in the metaverse, people can present themselves however they feel confident doing so, which is empowering and emboldening. These new, hyper personal communication models can be more authentic, and thus more trust-building, than face-to-face conversations, which are often stifled by social anxieties and power differentials. Early studies show that computer-mediated communication leads to higher productivity, saves time and money, connects people around the globe with ease, and fosters cooperation."

As mentioned earlier in this chapter, AI will be a major factor. But it will not just be about creating more immersive experience. The metaverse can actually improve the results of AI. For example, it can allow for better predictions, such as with the need for maintenance for equipment.

---

[26] https://business.oculus.com/case-studies/johnson-and-johnson/?utm_source=https%253A%252F%252Fwww.google.com%252F&utm_medium=organicsearch
[27] From the author's interview with Rebecca Binny on April 17, 2022.

"The biggest opportunity for the metaverse is the massive flow of data from the real world into the metaverse and back into the real world," said Lange. "It is this flywheel of data enriched with AI that will enable continuous improvement to the metaverse experience."

The metaverse will certainly have a major impact on ecommerce. In fact, it may ultimately challenge the seemingly invincible Amazon.

"While it was very difficult for people to envision back during the 1990s that the internet would transform commerce, there were a few companies and entrepreneurs that decided to make investments early," said George Korizis, who is the Customer Transformation Leader at PwC US.[28] "Those were the ones that received the dividends when the world implemented e-commerce and social media. Something similar will happen with the metaverse and businesses will soon realize that this is not just another marketing channel. We are seeing the beginning of a deep and significant transformation that will touch every sector of the economy."

But of course, there will be challenges. Again, there needs to be much more investment in software, infrastructure, and gear. But privacy will be another important consideration. With the Metaverse, you might be better able to detect the behavior of employees or customers. So, what can you do with the information?

Well, it seems like a good bet that there will be restrictions.

"Establishing trust must be a foundational element throughout every business' metaverse journey," said Korizis. "To cultivate trust among consumers, shareholders, regulators and other stakeholders, communicate early what to expect from your metaverse initiatives and how you will mitigate potential risks."

As for the rest of the chapter, we'll look at some other interesting startups in the metaverse space.

Genies

Akash Nigam's parents made an offer to him: either stay in college or raise $3 million.[29] Yes, he went on to raise the capital and launched a company called Blend, which was a messaging app.

While it was an interesting idea, it actually did not get much traction. Yet Nigam did not give up. He pivoted to another startup: Genies.

---

[28] This is from the author's interview with George Korizis on April 17, 2022.
[29] www.allamericanspeakers.com/celebritytalentbios/Akash+Nigam/435885

This one was the jackpot. Started in 2017, it was an early player in the creation of avatars. The timing was definitely spot-on. Genies was able to capitalize on the NFT revolution. But the metaverse is another big opportunity.

Being based in LA has been very helpful. It has allowed Genies to create avatars for celebrities like Justin Bieber, Shawn Mendes, Rihanna, Migos, Cardi B, J-Lo, and Offset. This not only validated the concept but helped get lots of distribution. There was also an important partnership with Warner Music Group.

Keep in mind that Genies avatars are not the typical ones seen in sticker packs, which are 2D animations. Instead, they are immersive and 3D. Users can also port their avatars to other platforms. This is possible because of the Genies SDK (Software Development Kit).

As a testament to the traction of Genies, the company was able to snag Robert Iger for its board of directors. This was his first move after retiring as the CEO and Chairman of the Walt Disney Co. During his tenure, he struck deals for companies like Marvel Entertainment, Lucasfilm, and Pixar.

According to Iger: "Imagine, you know, letting someone buy a Mickey Mouse avatar and customizing it in a way that not only would we never allow it before, but it was kind of hard to do in the physical world."[30]

In early 2022, Genies announced a $150 million round of funding.[31] The lead investor was Silver Lake. The valuation came to about $1 billion.

Now.gg

While the metaverse is often associated with immersive worlds and wearing VR headsets, the fact is that much of the action is with mobile apps. True, the experience is not necessarily the same. But it is getting more visual and realistic.

This is where now.gg is looking for opportunities. The CEO and founder is Rosen Sharma, who is a veteran of Silicon Valley. He has founded other companies like Game.tv and BlueStacks. He has also been an executive at large operators like McAfee.

As for now.gg, it is a global platform-as-a-service for game developers. It helps them create their own communities for any device or OS. The experiences can also be shared on social media channels. Then there is the ability for in-game payments.

---

[30] www.wsj.com/articles/after-walt-disney-robert-iger-heads-to-the-metaverse-11647259201
[31] https://techcrunch.com/2022/04/12/avatar-startup-genies-hits-1-billion-valuation-in-latest-raise/

Now.gg has built the Creator Studio and Creator hub. They allow mobile gamers to modify their games, such as with changing colors, visual effects and adding textures. For the most part, this will be key for the metaverse.

"Today, over five billion people have access to mobile phones and half of those people are mobile gamers," said Sharma.[32] "In addition to the behaviors of literally billions of people, my own daughters were an incredible source of inspiration. They are always playing and sharing games with ease, and I thought there had to be a way to enable anyone, anywhere, on any device to play and share mobile games with this kind of ease."

He is also developing systems for NFGs or non-fungible games. This is actually a way to transition games to Web3 and the metaverse.

"NFGs enable the unbundling of game code, events, and art to create multiple versions of games," said Sharma. "This ability to unbundle - on a mobile cloud - opens up tremendous opportunities for developers to create and build on top of existing businesses. For example, users can find and use NFTs in the game and create an entirely personalized game experience by collecting NFT or non-NFT based 2D and 3D images, textures, videos and code."

Teslasuit

Sergei Nossoff has over 20 years as an executive and founder of tech companies.[33] He also has a background as an investor.

But he thinks that the next-big-thing will be the metaverse. And yes, this is the focus of his latest startup: Teslasuit. The company develops whole-body haptic feedback and climate control suits. Thus, they allow for a person to be completely in the metaverse.

The technology is certainly complex. Here's a look at the main components:

- Haptic Feedback: The technology is built throughout the whole suit. As a result, the user gets the sensation of touch within a virtual environment.

- Biometrics: This monitors a user's health and performance data. They can measure stress levels and emotional states. Because of this, a VR system can adapt the content based on the experience of the user.

---

[32] This is from the author's interview with Rosen Sharma on April 18, 2022.
[33] www.linkedin.com/in/nossoff/?originalSubdomain=uk

- Motion Capture: This records and tracks body positions and movements. This is done by using an integrated skeletal and 3D kinematic motion system.

One of Teslasuit's first customers is NASA.[34] The space agency has purchased Developer Kits to help improve the cognitive and physical performance of astronauts.

Another customer is DTEK, which is an electricity producer. The company uses Teslasuits for inspections and repairs for its power plants. The result was a 30% decline in error rates.

Conclusion

The metaverse has been around for a long time. But with Meta's huge investments in the category, this technology has become red hot. Other megatech operators like Apple and Microsoft are gunning for the opportunity as well.

The metaverse will take considerable time to evolve. It may easily be more than a decade of effort. But then again, this is where entrepreneurs can play a big role. They can help with the many technologies that must be built.

For example, there will be a need for systems to allow for haptic feedback, so as to make experiences more realistic. There will also be a need to create tools that allow for the creation of virtual items and new worlds. AI will also be a critical factor for the success of the metaverse. Oh, and then there will be the demand for more advanced infrastructure solutions, such as for edge computing.

Currently, much of the activity with the metaverse is with gaming and consumer applications. However, it looks like the enterprise interest is rising. Thus, the total market opportunity for the metaverse is likely to be huge.

As for the next chapter, we'll take a look at taxes and regulations for Web3.

---

[34] https://teslasuit.io/special/TESLASUIT-presentation-Q12021.pdf

Taxes and Regulations

How to Navigate the Web3 World

Brian Armstrong, who is the cofounder and CEO of Coinbase, has noted: "My belief is that the vast majority of people using digital currency today are not seeking to evade taxes. They are simply investors seeking returns and people interested in a nascent new technology."[1]

This seems like a reasonable assessment. Yet taxes are certainly a major consideration with the crypto world. A big issue is that there remains uncertainty – and this can make it difficult for businesses to operate.

Consider a survey from CoinTracker. When it was taken – on March 27, 2022 – about 96% of the respondents still had not filed their tax returns and 75% said they were not ready to do so.[2] The survey also showed that many people could not assess the correct approach to taxes for typical crypto transactions.

---

[1] www.brainyquote.com/quotes/brian_armstrong_851355?src=t_taxes
[2] www.cnbc.com/2022/04/06/most-cryptocurrency-investors-still-arent-ready-to-file-their-taxes.html

© Tom Taulli 2022
T. Taulli, *How to Create a Web3 Startup*,
https://doi.org/10.1007/978-1-4842-8683-8_9

So, in this chapter, we'll get an overview of this topic. Again, it is subject to change. Keep in mind that the IRS still has not ruled on various important issues. The same goes for many states.

For this chapter, we'll also take a look at regulations for Web3 and the focus will be on the United States.

Crypto Taxes

In 2021, the IRS ramped up its efforts with crypto transactions. This was certainly evident with the new 1040 form. There is the following question: "At any time during 2021, did you receive, sell, exchange, or otherwise dispose of any financial interest in any virtual currency?"[3]

On its face, this seems straightforward. But the question has vague aspects. For example, what does it mean to "receive" virtual currency? Is this from a gift or the issuance from a company or an inheritance? It's not clear.

Something else: What is "any financial interest"? Do you need to own it? Or does it mean something else – like a sharing arrangement?

Again, it's far from clear.

Then what to do? When it comes to taxes on crypto, there often is a need for judgment calls. This is why it is important to get the advice of a qualified CPA (Certified Public Account) or Enrolled Agent (EA). They will know how to interpret the tax laws but also provide guidance on what the IRS is looking for.

Tax Scenarios

Note that the IRS ruled – in 2014 – that cryptocurrency represents property. It is not treated as fiat currency like the US dollar or the euro.

This has major consequences. Basically, the IRS considers cryptocurrencies to be an investment like stocks or bonds.

Let's take a look. Suppose you pay $30,000 for one Bitcoin. This is your "cost basis" in the property. Within six months, the value of your Bitcoin hits $50,000 and you sell your coin. The IRS considers this a capital gain of $20,000 or $50,000 minus $30,000. Since you made the transaction within a year or less, it's treated as a short-term capital gain. This means that you pay the same taxes as you would with your ordinary income, such as your salary.

---

[3] www.irs.gov/pub/irs-pdf/f1040.pdf

You can deduct for any fees. For example, an exchange will charge a commission of 2% to 5% on the transaction. You will add this to the cost basis, which will reduce your taxes. Using our example, suppose the fee is 3%. In this case, the amount you add to the cost basis will be $600 or 3% multiplied by $20,000. The capital gain will come to $29,400 or $50,000 minus $20,600.

■ **Note**   It does not matter if you sold your cryptocurrency for another one, say Ether. There will still be a taxable transaction.

OK, what if you sold your coin after a year? In this case, you have a long-term capital gain. You will pay the favorable tax rates for this transaction. The maximum is 20% versus 37% for ordinary income.

On the other hand, suppose you generate a loss on the transaction. This will be a capital loss and you can offset this against any of your gains. After doing this, if you still have a net loss, you can deduct up to $3,000 against your ordinary income each year. You can do this until you have no more capital losses.

True, all this seems standard. But the hard part is when you use cryptocurrency to make a purchase of product or service.

Here's an example. You agree to buy a Tesla by using two Bitcoins, which add up to $80,000. But there is a problem. You may owe taxes on this transaction!

How so? Let's take a look. Suppose that you bought two Bitcoins for $60,000. As a result, the purchase of the Tesla actually represents a "sale" of these coins, and you owe taxes on a $20,000 capital gain.

This is a big reason why it is difficult to use cryptocurrencies for ordinary purchases. This can mean complex tax problems. Then again, this is why stablecoins have become popular. With less volatility in their prices, the taxes' implications are not as significant.

With cryptocurrency, you may receive income as well. This could be interest or even an airdrop. When this happens, the IRS considers this to be ordinary income and you will have to pay taxes on it.

Another scenario is if you receive cryptocurrency for services. This could be as an employee or contractor. Regardless, the value of the cryptocurrency will be ordinary income and taxable.

However, many people may not report this. Part of this is the common perception that − since there is no cash exchanged − there is no legal requirement. Or it could be that it would be difficult for the IRS to track this. But none of these reasons are valid. You are required to pay taxes.

An area that appears to be a loophole is with the "wash rule." For stocks and bonds, this means you cannot recognize a capital loss if you sell and buy back the security – or a similar asset – after 30 days. However, this rule does not apply with cryptocurrencies. Yet this may not last long. Congress has been considering a change.

When you make transactions with stocks, bonds, and other securities, your brokerage firm will provide you a 1099-B from. This will itemize and summarize the transactions, which makes it easier to prepare your taxes.

What about cryptocurrency? This is voluntary for exchanges. But by 2023, they will be required to issue 1099s. This will make it much easier for the IRS to track taxpayers and enforce the laws.

Consider that there are Individual Retirement Accounts (IRAs) that allow you to invest in crypto. You do not pay taxes on the transactions until you withdraw the money. Some of the IRA providers include Kingdom Trust and BitcoinIRA.[4]

Large financial institutions are also eyeing the massive retirement market. Take a look at Fidelity. In early 2022, the company announced plans to offer Bitcoin as an investment for its 401(k)s. Fidelity is the largest provider of retirement plans, which has over 20 million participants.[5]

But the U.S. Labor Department has shown skepticism. The agency has indicated that employers should "exercise extreme care."[6]

NFT Taxes

For the most part, NFT taxes are treated in a similar way to cryptocurrencies. The IRS considers both to be property.

However, with NFTs, the rules are even more opaque. The reason is that the IRS has provided fairly limited guidance on the tax regulations. This is primarily due to the fact that NFTs are new.

First of all, let's take a look at taxes for buying and selling NFTs. You will often use Ether for these transactions. Thus, when you make a purchase, there may be a capital gain or loss for the cryptocurrency. Then you will have the same for the transaction of the NFT – which could be a long or short-term capital gain.

---

[4] www.wsj.com/articles/saving-for-retirement-now-you-can-bet-on-bitcoin-11624613435
[5] www.wsj.com/articles/fidelity-to-allow-retirement-savers-to-put-bitcoin-in-401-k-accounts-11650945661
[6] www.wsj.com/articles/fidelity-to-allow-retirement-savers-to-put-bitcoin-in-401-k-accounts-11650945661

But there is a wrinkle to consider. The IRS has not ruled on what type of gain or loss is available for an NFT. This asset could actually be treated as a collectible. If so, this means that the maximum tax rate is 28%, compared to the 20% rate for a long-term capital gain. In fact, it seems that the IRS is likely to lean toward NFTs as collectibles. But again, you should seek advice from a qualified tax professional.

Next, there are tax considerations for those who create NFTs. This could be about an artist who uses a tool to make the smart contract and then uploads the NFT to a marketplace.

The creation of this digital asset has no tax consequences. It's only when you sell it. In these cases, it is considered ordinary income. You will also have to pay self-employment taxes. This is your share for Social Security, Medicare, and state benefits programs. And this tax can add up. For Social Security, the tax rate is 12.4% of net earnings (up to $142,800 of earnings are subject to this tax) and is 2.9% for Medicare (there is no cap on this). If you make $200,000 as single filer or $250,000 as a married couple with a joint return, there is an extra 0.9% Medicare tax.

The IRS will consider you as a contractor. As a result, you will file a Schedule C form. You will list your earnings and deduct any qualified business expenses. This could be fees, gas, subscriptions, software, and so on.

The creator may earn ongoing income. This could be the result of the number of viewers of the NFT, the royalties, commissions for sales of the NFT, and interest. All this is considered ordinary income and is taxable.

Then what about when an NFT is given away? This is generally for the purposes of a marketing campaign. But for those who receive the NFT, there may be a tax consequence. The key is there must be value to this digital asset.

And this may be tough to determine. The fact is that there may be little to no value. Although, if the NFT is resold on a marketplace, then this would be probably the best indication that there is value to it.

Donations

Donating cryptocurrency and NFTs has become much more popular. This is definitely a unique way of helping a cause. For example, when Russia invaded Ukraine, there was a surge in cryptocurrency donations.

Of course, there are tax and estate planning advantages. When you make the donation, there is no taxable event. What's more, if you hold onto the digital asset for over one year and you itemize your deductions, you can deduct up to 30% of your AGI (Adjusted Gross Income). For amounts over this, you can carry them forward for up to five years.

If you hold onto the cryptocurrency for one year or less and you itemize deductions, you can deduct the lesser of the cost basis or fair market value of the digital asset. The amount for the donation is up to 50% and there is a five-year period for carryforwards.

For each of these, you need to file a Form 8283. If the amount of the donation or gift is over $5,000, you will need to obtain a third-party appraisal.

While all of this can be beneficial for your taxes, there is a problem. The fact is that many charities and nonprofits do not accept cryptocurrency donations.

True, you can sell your cryptocurrency and then make the donation. But of course, you may be subject to paying a tax on the gains.

The IRS

The IRS is the world's largest collection agency. It has significant powers, such as to seize your property, subpoena your records, or even incarcerate you.

In light of all this, you really need to be mindful of the tax issues of cryptocurrencies. It's easy to make mistakes – and yes, these can be costly. Consider that the fines can be hefty.

You should also keep track of your records. So if there is an IRS audit, you will be prepared to make your case. This will go a long way in minimizing or avoiding any adverse impacts.

However, if you do get a notice from the IRS, then the best policy is to seek the help of a tax professional.

Cybersecurity and Regulations

The risk of cybersecurity breaches is perhaps the biggest drivers for regulation. Granted, the security for Bitcoin and other core blockchains are extremely strong. The problem is the security issues with systems and applications built on top of platforms. For the most part, breaches and hacks have become more prevalent.

A notable case is the Axie Infinity virtual world, which involves large amounts of transactions for NFTs. In 2022, the company notified its users that there was a hack for over $600 million.[7] It was actually the second largest in crypto history.

---

[7] www.nbcnews.com/tech/tech-news/hackers-steal-600-million-maker-axie-infinity-rcna22031

The hackers were able to take control of the Ronin system, which powers Axie Infinity. Yet the company took six days to find out about this.[8] But of course, it was too late.

Axie Infinity scrambled to raise $150 million in capital from investors like Binance, Animoca Brands, a16z, Dialectic, Paradigm, and Accel.[9] The company said it planned to use its own money to reimburse users as well.

They also initiated a major upgrade of the platform and increased the number of validators for the DAO. There will be more frequent audits.

Despite all this, the event was a shocker for the Web3 community. The investors in the $150 million round were trying to shore up some trust. But ultimately, if the hacks continue, it seems likely that there will be increased regulation of the industry.

■ **Note**　According to research from Chainalysis, criminals stole about $14 billion of crypto in 2021, up from $7.8 billion in the year before.[10]

What Crypto Regulation Might Look Like?

In early 2022, President Biden announced his executive order about cryptocurrency. It was called "Ensuring Responsible Development of Digital Assets."[11]

The document did not provide any new regulations or requirements. Instead, it was about directing federal agencies to study the cryptocurrency market and provide recommendations.

It was a sensible approach. The market is very complicated and evolving. Besides, it looks like the Administration does not want to impose undue burdens. The United States has been a leader in global finance for decades. And cryptocurrencies are likely to be important to continuing this leadership.

However, the Administration recognizes the needs for guardrails. The industry also seems to be generally in support of this. If there are not sufficient consumer protections, the growth of the crypto market could easily stall.

---

[8] https://techcrunch.com/2022/04/07/why-binance-led-the-axie-infinity-bailout-and-what-it-means-for-cryptos-future/
[9] https://cointelegraph.com/news/axie-infinity-creator-raises-150m-led-by-binance-to-reimburse-stolen-funds
[10] https://time.com/nextadvisor/investing/cryptocurrency/why-crypto-regulation-is-good-for-investors/
[11] www.wsj.com/articles/biden-to-order-study-of-cryptocurrency-risk-creation-of-u-s-digital-currency-11646823600

If anything, the situation is similar to the 1920s. At this time, there was significant speculation in the stock market. But this led to excessive risks, such as with borrowing against stock.

When the market crashed in 1929, this helped to ignite the Great Depression. The result was that the stock market saw muted activity for years. To help encourage more confidence, the Roosevelt Administration passed several pieces of legislation that introduced the federal securities laws. The Securities and Exchange Commission (SEC) was set up to enforce them. The main goal was to require that companies provide enough disclosures for investors to make prudent decisions. This was through documents like prospectuses.

In the case with crypto, it seems unlikely that there will be a new agency created. The SEC may ultimately be the main one to enforce any new laws. Or it could be a coordination with other agencies.

But it seems likely there will be some requirement for more detailed disclosures. This would also be backed up with third-party audits.

There will also likely be industry-specific regulations, especially in areas like healthcare and financial services. There are certainly major issues with privacy. For example, with a healthcare company, it could be difficult to use the Ethereum blockchain. If it is shared with multiple companies, this could actually be a violation of the antitrust laws.

Something else: Since crypto is a global industry, there is a need to understand the regulations in other countries. They may ultimately be more restrictive outside the United States. As a result, it can be difficult to roll out an application.

Note   In Biden's executive order on crypto, there is a provision that explores the development of a digital currency for the United States. This could have important benefits, such as lower costs and quick settlements. But developing this would likely be challenging. Treasury Secretary Janet Yellen said it could take years to create one.[12]

When it comes to crypto regulation, a guide to what might happen is to look at the New York State Department of Financial Services. The organization regulates many of the world's largest financial institutions.

---

[12] www.wsj.com/articles/crypto-like-digital-dollar-at-least-several-years-away-yellen-says-11649353558?mod=lead_feature_below_a_pos1

An important initiative is to encourage companies to use analytics software for compliance, such as with anti-money-laundering laws.[13] In traditional finance, these tools have been incredibly helpful. The same should be the case with crypto. If anything, it may help to lower the costs of compliance because part of the process will be automated.

Some VCs are even creating their own position papers for shaping regulation. An example is Andreessen Horowitz. The firm released a document entitled, "How to Build a Better Internet: 10 Principles for World Leaders Shaping the Future of Web3."[14]

They include the following:

- Establish a clear vision to foster a decentralized digital infrastructure.

- Embrace multi-stakeholder approaches to governance and regulation.

- Create targeted, risk-calibrated oversight regimes for different Web3 activities.

- Foster innovation with composability, open-source code, and the power of open communities.

- Broaden access to the economic benefits of the innovation economy.

- Unlock the potential of DAOs

- Deploy web3 to further sustainability goals.

- Embrace the role of well-regulated stablecoins in financial inclusion and innovation.

- Collaborate with other nations to harmonize standards and regulatory frameworks.

- Provide clear, fair tax rules for the reporting of digital assets, and leverage technical solutions for tax compliance.

---

[13] www.wsj.com/articles/crypto-firms-should-use-blockchain-analytics-new-york-regulator-says-11651186279?mod=hp_minor_pos11
[14] https://a16z.com/2022/01/07/how-to-build-a-better-internet-10-principles-for-world-leaders-shaping-the-future-of-web3/

Lawyers and Lobbyists

For traditional financial services companies, there is usually a large legal department. The same is happening in the crypto world. These firms realize that they need much better protection. They are also looking at anticipating potential regulations.

The result is that the recruiting for lawyers seems at par with that of finding top-notch developers. There is a low supply of experienced legal experts available. This is definitely driving up compensation packages. Some can be seven figures. By comparison, a top federal regulator's salary comes to about $250,000.[15]

However, hiring lawyers could be cheaper. By comparison, retaining a law firm can be even more expensive.

But this move is also being driven by investors. They want a better legal foundation – and this can be easier with in-house talent.

Crypto firms are also hiring lobbyists and former regulators. For example, Crypto.com hired Duncan DeVille as the executive vice president for compliance.[16] Before this, he was an executive at Western Union and an official at the U.S. Treasury Department's financial crimes unit.

■ **Note**   The chief compliance officer at Kracken – Marco Santori – tweeted that he was looking to hire 30 lawyers within three months. But he would have preferred 60 but said he didn't know how to "get it done."[17]

Then again, the consequences for compliance violations can be significant. Just look at the situation with BlockFi Lending. The company settled with the Securities and Exchange Commission (SEC) for $100 million.[18] This was the largest payout in the cryptocurrency industry. The company has since introduced a new account that meets SEC rules, such as with the filing of a registration statement.

In another case, Coinbase attempted to introduce a lending product. Although, the SEC said it would file a lawsuit over it. Coinbase would eventually pullback.

---

[15] www.wsj.com/articles/crypto-aims-to-boost-influence-with-washington-hires-11647042604?mod=hp_lead_pos1
[16] www.wsj.com/articles/crypto-com-hires-financial-crimes-expert-from-western-union-11649707396?mod=hp_minor_pos10
[17] www.wsj.com/articles/crypto-industry-cant-hire-enough-lawyers-11650879002?mod=hp_lista_pos5
[18] www.wsj.com/articles/blockfi-to-pay-record-penalty-to-settle-sec-probe-of-crypto-lending-business-11644854400?mod=article_inline

The SEC is likely to get more aggressive. In 2022, the federal agency announced that it planned to double its staff to regulate the cryptocurrency markets.

At a Senate Banking Committee hearing, SEC chairman Gary Gensler said: "Currently, we just don't have enough investor protection in crypto finance, issuance, trading, or lending. Frankly, at this time, it's more like the Wild West or the old world of 'buyer beware' that existed before the securities laws were enacted."[19]

■ **Note**   Billionaire investor Warren Buffett is definitely no fan of crypto. At his 2022 Berkshire Hathaway Annual Shareholder meeting, he said the following about Bitcoin: "Now if you told me you own all of the bitcoin in the world and you offered it to me for $25, I wouldn't take it because what would I do with it? I'd have to sell it back to you one way or another. It isn't going to do anything. Assets, to have value, have to deliver something to somebody."[20]

For the rest of the chapter, we'll look at some of the interesting startups in the Web3 finance and cybersecurity markets.

CertiK

Ronghui Gu grew up in China. While in high school, he won the national first prize in the Olympiad math competition, which allowed him to attend the distinguished Tsinghua University.[21] Yet he was not interested in majoring in math. He instead wanted to focus on computer programming.

He would eventually get a Ph.D. in Computer Science at Yale and become a professor at Columbia University. While there, he met Yale Computer Science professor Zhong Shao. They struck up a friendship and would work together on areas like cybersecurity.

In 2018, they saw an opportunity in the blockchain space and founded CertiK. It was based on cutting-edge technology called Formal Verification. This allows for a high degree of security for both hardware and software systems. It involves using complex math and algorithms to prove the satisfaction of requirements and specifications. For example, each step in a process is explained. And since it is based purely on math, you do not have to place trust on a third party, such as a security consultant.

---

[19] www.cnbc.com/2022/05/03/sec-adds-to-cryptocurrency-regulation-staff.html
[20] www.cnbc.com/2022/04/30/warren-buffett-gives-his-most-expansive-explanation-for-why-he-doesnt-believe-in-bitcoin.html
[21] https://medium.com/foothill-ventures/founders-lessons-ronghui-gu-of-certik-53c39c76e3b8

CertiK has been a major innovator in the Formal Verification space. The company has been the first to launch an OS kernel and cloud commodity hypervisor with this technology.

The technology can be applied to areas outside of blockchain and Web3. Just some include autonomous driving, IoT (Internet of Things), and cloud computing. In other words, the market opportunity is enormous.

However, the main focus for CertiK is on Web3 – and it has definitely been the right choice. In early 2022, the company raised $88 million at a $2 billion valuation. Some of the investors included Tiger Global, Goldman Sachs, and Sequoia Capital. In all, the company has raised $230 million.

The CertiK platform protects over $300 billion in crypto assets across 2,500 enterprises.[22] In 2021, the revenues soared by 12X, and the profits increased by 3,000X.

LiquiFi

A cap table – or capitalization table – is a list of the securities and who owns them. For startups, they usually include common stock, preferred stock, convertible notes, and employee stock options. The cap table is crucial when it comes to understanding the valuation of a startup as well as for managing a fundraise.

But with Web3 companies, it can be much more complex. There needs to be a way to track tokens and their values. There may also be complex structures with DAOs.

What to do? Well, LiquiFi has built an online platform to manage the cap table for Web3 companies. Some of the features include vesting of contracts and employee stock options, tax compliance and reporting, and the enablement of tokens for staking. The company also provides consulting for clients.

The founders of the company are Robin Ji, who is the CEO, and Oliver Tang, who is the CTO. They came up with the idea because of their first-hand experience working with crypto companies.[23] The founders got their initial backing from Y Combinator in the winter of 2021.

The company is currently on Ethereum and Polygon. But there are plans to expand on to other blockchains.

---

[22] https://techcrunch.com/2022/04/07/goldman-sachs-joins-other-investors-in-88m-round-for-web3-and-blockchain-security-firm-certik/

[23] https://techcrunch.com/2022/04/21/liquifi-is-building-carta-web3-for-crypto-companies-tokens-blockchain/

In early 2022, LiquiFi raised $5 million in a seed round.[24] Some of the investors were Alliance DAO, Robot Ventures, Y Combinator, and Orange DAO.

Conclusion

In this chapter, we got an overview of taxes and regulations for the crypto industry. In terms of taxes, they are still somewhat vague. This is especially the case with NFTs.

But the IRS is likely to provide more guidance in the years ahead. The agency is also investing heavily in enforecement actions against potential fraud in the crypto industry.

In this chapter, we also took a look at the potential for regulations. For Web3, the environment is still fairly wide open. But there are already indications that the federal government will look at ways to impose regulations. However, crypto companies and VCs are bolstering their lobbying efforts.

We are also at the end of the book. We have certainly covered a lot. The industry is still in the early phases. But with this book, you will have a much better foundation – in terms of the core technologies, trends, and issues.

So good luck on your Web3 journey. It will definitely be exciting!

---

[24]www.aliens.com/livenews/latest/web3-startup-liquifi-closes-dollar5-million-round-led-by-dragonfly-capital-partners

G

Glossary

Airdrop: This refers to when a Web3 project gives away tokens. It's also possible to airdrop NFTs. Often, this is to encourage people to sign up for a project.

Altcoin: This is essentially any cryptocurrency other than Bitcoin. Since the blockchain is open source, it has been easy to create altcoins. There are thousands on the market. However, during the past few years, the use of "altcoin" has been losing favor.

Audit Protocols: These are guidelines for ensuring stability for smart contracts.

Avatar: This is your visual representation in a virtual environment, like the metaverse.

Backend Developer: This is someone who focuses on the server-side of an application. This often means using or writing APIs.

Bitcoin: This is the first viable cryptocurrency, which is based on blockchain technology. Bitcoin remains the most valuable cryptocurrency. The technology is based on a whitepaper written by Satoshi Nakamoto, which was published in 2008.

Block: This is a group of data that is on the blockchain. When a block is created, the system will make a 32-bit number called a nonce. This will make the header.

Blockchain: This is a public database that is openly distributed on the Internet. Data and applications are added to it through the use of cryptography, such as with the use of private and public keys.

© Tom Taulli 2022
T. Taulli, *How to Create a Web3 Startup*,
https://doi.org/10.1007/978-1-4842-8683-8

Brownie Framework: This is a framework based on Python and provides for creating smart contracts on Ethereum. For the development, you can use Solidity or Vyper.

Cold Wallet: This is a physical device that stores crypto. An example is a thumb drive.

Collector DAOs: These are generally for NFTs that represent albums, artwork, and videos. Some of the Collector DAOs include Flamingo DAO and PleasrDAO.

Community Manager: This is a person that helps to grow and evolve a startup's community. This is often done by using social media, events, blogs, and educational resources.

Composability: This is a technology that is in the form of a component. It's similar to an API (Application Programming Interface). In terms of Web3, composability means you can build an application like putting together a set of Legos.

Creator DAO: This is a platform for super fans, such as for a music group. Usually, the DAO will issue an NFT. This can provide benefits like VIP passes, discounts on merchandise, and early access to events.

Decentralization: This is a technology architecture that does not have a central authority or intermediaries. Instead, there are peer-to-peer transactions with users.

Decentralized Autonomous Organization (DAO): This is an entity that manages a Web3 project or platform. There is no traditional structure like a board of directors. Instead, the DAO operates based on the voting of crypto tokens.

DeFi or Decentralized Finance: This is a peer-to-peer system for financial transactions. There are usually lower costs, less paperwork, and faster settlements.

Developer Advocate: This is a person who cultivates the relationships for a company's developers. This role is generally for infrastructure and tools companies in the Web3 space.

Developer Grants: This is a way to encourage coders to come on board a project. The grant could be in the form of tokens or traditional money.

Decentralized Exchange (DEX): This is a marketplace for trading US dollars and other fiat currencies for cryptocurrencies.

Divisibility: This means you can divide a currency or cryptocurrency into other denominations. An example is converting a ten-dollar bill into ten one-dollar bills.

Dynamic Application Security Testing (DAST): This is about looking for security vulnerabilities by simulating attacks while an application is running.

Ethereum: This is a blockchain platform. It allows for the creation of smart contracts, which are often used for developing Web3 apps.

Ethereum Virtual Machine (EVM): This translates the code into bytecode and then is put on the blockchain.

Ethers.js: This is a library that uses JavaScript and TypeScript to provide four main modules to interact with Ethereum.

Externally Owned Accounts (EOA): This is used to setup an Ethereum account. You have control with a private key and there is no code with it. You can send ether or messages from this account.

Frontend Developer: This is someone who focuses on the UI of a website or mobile app. The skills for the person usually involve both design and scripting.

Gas: This is a fee for using Ethereum. You pay for it using the Ether coin.

Governance Token: This is an altcoin that provides a mechanism for voting on a blockchain project. This type of token is what is often used for DeFi systems.

Halving: For Bitcoin, this is where every four years, the number of new coins gets reduced by 50%.

Hard Fork: This is where there is a clear split in the blockchain and there is no longer backwards compatibility. This is when there will be the creation of a new cryptocurrency.

Hardhat: This is a framework that allows you to create a marketplace – with little work. This handles all the complex matters of managing digital assets. The framework supports Django and Ruby on Rails frameworks.

Hot Wallet: This is where you store the cryptocurrency on an exchange.

Impermanent Loss: This is a temporary loss for a DeFi system. This often happens because of imbalances with supply-and-demand in the marketplace.

IoT (Internet of Things): This is the network of physical nodes, such as sensors. This allows connections for the Internet to exchange information. Examples include smart appliances, industrial systems, and self-driving cars.

Interoperability: This means you can use the NFT for other platforms.

Layer 1: This is the core infrastructure for the blockchain. It involves the underlying network, hardware, and connections.

Layer 2: These are Web3 solutions that help to increase the speed of transactions.

Layer 3: This is the application layer for Web 3. This is where programs like dApps operate.

Mainnet: This is a Web3 project that is available to the public.

Memecoins: These are altcoins that are more about fun and entertainment. Interestingly, some of them started as mere jokes.

Metaverse: This is a highly immersive online experience. It's essentially a virtual world that is very realistic.

Miner: This is a computer that processes huge amounts of data to verify new blocks on the blockchain. Common ways of doing this include solving for proof of work (PoW) or proof of stake (PoS).

Nodes: These are the computers on the blockchain network. They will provide the compute power to create and verify new blocks.

Non-Fungible Tokens (NFTs): This a technology, which is based on blockchain, that allows people to own digital items.

oo7.js: This is a library that uses expressions or bonds. This essentially makes it possible to understand when values are triggered on a smart contract for Ethereum.

OpenZeppelin SDK: This is a framework built on the Python language and provides components for NFTs and other tokens. It has sophisticated security systems built in.

Option Pool: This is an allocation of a startup's equity devoted to equity compensation, such as with stock options. The percentage often ranges from 5% to 25% of the outstanding shares.

Permissionless: This means that anyone can use a technology without having to create login credentials or to get authorization from a central provider.

Private Blockchain: This is a blockchain that has a central authority that grants access to users. A private blockchain is often used by businesses that need privacy.

Private Key: This is a long string of characters that is essentially a password. It allows you to access your crypto assets.

Protocol DAO: This is a project that is focused on leveraging Ethereum for DeFi applications. Some examples include Aaave, Compound, and MakerDAO.

Provenance: This is a history of who has owned an NFT. This can provide insight on the value of the item.

Public Benefit Corporation (PBC): This is a new type of corporation – which is recognized by Delaware law – that is focused on ESG (Environment, Social, and Governance) values.

Public Key: This is a long string of characters. Think of it like an email address. It is where you can send cryptocurrencies to someone else.

Remix: This is a popular IDE (Integrated Development Environment) for Web3 development. The systems are built to allow for the writing, running, debugging, and deploying of smart contracts on the blockchain. There is also seamless integration with the Ethereum Virtual Machine (EVM).

Restricted Stock: This is stock issued to employees of the startup. However, there are vesting requirements.

Rug Pulls: This is where a Web3 developer abandons a project and takes the money. There can be little recourse for those who have been defrauded.

Rust: This is a computer language that is object oriented and is similar to C++. It can process large amounts of data and has proven effective with developing Web3 applications.

Security Tokens: These allow you to acquire interests like real estate, artwork, or other physical assets. The ownership can also be fractional.

Smart Contract: This is an application that is on a blockchain. This allows for NFTs and DeFi applications.

Social DAO: This is a platform with a strong community element. Some of the DAOs in this category are Seed Club, Friends with Benefits, and FiatLuxDAO.

Soft Fork: This is an upgrade to the existing blockchain, and the network's users must approve it. There also needs to be backwards combability with the existing forks.

Solana: This is an alternative to Ethereum. This blockchain provides for smart contracts and can be used to create non-fungible tokens (NFTs) and decentralized applications (dApps).

Solidity: This is a popular language for Web3 development. It is similar to C++ and has object-oriented features. Besides Ethereum, you can use Solidity for other platforms like Tron, Hedera Hashgraph, Avalanche, and Binance Smart Chain.

Stablecoin: This is an altcoin whose value is connected to another asset, such as gold or a fiat currency.

Staking: This is using cryptocurrency as collateral for the possibility of validating blocks on the blockchain. This is a way to show the level of commitment of the user.

Static Analysis (SAST): This is automated analysis of source code without executing the application.

Stock Option: This gives you the right to buy a fixed number of shares at a fixed price for a period of time.

Testnet: This is an instance of a blockchain that you can test software. There is no risk of losing funds. Rather, there are testnet coins that do not have any value.

TradeFi: This refers to traditional financial services companies like banks, investment banks, and brokerages.

Transaction Throughput: This refers to the transactions per second for a blockchain system.

Truffle: This is a framework that has easy-to-use tools for creating, debugging and deploying smart contracts for Ethereum. It also has integrations with popular Web frameworks like React, Angular, and Vue.

TVL (Total Value Locked): This is a key metric for a DeFi system. This measures the total amount of assets for a protocol or network.

Utility Tokens: These are altcoins often used for online services.

Vesting: This is where an employee must remain at a company for a certain period of time to earn equity or a stock option.

Vyper: This is a language used for developing smart contracts for the Ethereum Virtual Machine (EVM). A key advantage is its high levels of security.

Wallet: This is where you can store your crypto assets.

Wash Trading: A user is both the seller and buyer for a transaction. This is possible because you can easily create two wallets and not provide any identifying information. With wash trading, this can cause artificial volume in an NFT, which may attract interest.

Web1: This is the first era of the Internet. The roots go back to the 1960s. But it was not until the mid-1990s that Web1 became a part of the mainstream. A key was the use of open protocols like Transmission Control Protocol and Internet Protocol, or TCP/IP, Domain name system (DNS), SMTP, or the Simple Message Transfer Protocol, and File Transfer Protocol (FTP). They allowed for a decentralized way to build and use the Internet.

Web2: This emerged around 2004. The Internet became more about sharing and social networking. However, a handful of megatech companies would dominate the industry like Apple, Amazon, and Google.

Web3: This is the next generation of the Internet. It is based on a decentralized model. This means that users control their own data and also become owners in the platforms.

Web3.js: This is a Web3 library that allows for creating functions for on-chain transactions and components for Ethereum nodes. This basically makes it easier to handle the JSON RPC mechanism for the transmission of the data (this is a standard format).

Whitelisting: This is where a select group of people are invited to participate in a project. Then when it is launched to the public, they will derive significant gains.

Yield Farming: This is a service – based on a DEX – that searches for higher returns from various tokens.

Zero-Knowledge Proof (ZKP): This is where a user (the prover) can verify the information for another user (the verifier) without there being any more information disclosed.

Zinc: This is a framework that allows for the creation of smart contracts. Zinc is similar to the Rust language.

Index

I

© Tom Taulli 2022
T. Taulli, *How to Create a Web3 Startup*,
https://doi.org/10.1007/978-1-4842-8683-8

Printed in the United States
by Baker & Taylor Publisher Services